MW01028829

HE'S GOT MOVES

25 Legendary Chess Games
(As Analyzed by a Smart Kid)

Oliver Boydell

New York

Cover: Benjamin Alfonsi and Jason Snyder
Design: Erik Christopher

Published by Metabook, an imprint of Metabook Entertainment.

Metabook Inc.
375 Greenwich Street
New York, New York 10013
www.metabookentertainment.com

ISBN 978-0-9992119-6-0

For my mother, Thieulam

CONTENTS

FOREWORD

I first met Oliver Boydell early in 2016. This was shortly after he had captured the National Kindergarten Chess Championship some months before. He would soon distinguish himself further by winning the New York City First Grade Chess Championship. Clearly, he was a force on the move.

I then had an opportunity to sit down with Oliver and talk chess. I was struck by his enormous talent and tactical aptitude from the start. He made calculations accurately and quickly. It seemed he was solving combinations faster than I could set them up. And there was no end to it. He wanted to see more problems, and he wanted them to be harder.

The chess gods must have been smiling on both of us that day. Oliver had found someone who also loved chess, who was fascinated by its harmony and multifarious concepts. On my side of the equation, I had found an ardent, superlative, top-of-the-line student. Since then, we have continued to explore the beautiful patterns and proportioned symmetries of chess ideas together.

Now, Oliver has put his genius into a cohesive package: a one-of-a-kind chess book. He has crafted engaging text, with quality examples and instructive insights, all artfully presented and arranged. Spanning two centuries of premier gamesmanship – from the 1850s to 2020 – Oliver has assembled some of the world's best chess games into a superbly integrated volume.

I had never heard of a ten-year-old who had even attempted to write such a book, let alone complete it with panache and delightful humor. But that is exactly what Oliver Boydell has done. Here, in

He's Got Moves, with the enchanting subtitle, *25 Legendary Chess Games (As Analyzed by a Smart Kid)*, he offers a collection of edifying chess games, logically analyzed and incisively elucidated, framed in pragmatic, cogent language, and methodically diagrammed. To be sure, the principles of chess have rarely been rendered so charmingly accessible.

The format is simple and to the point. Each game is introduced with a descriptive caption and an informative paragraph. The illuminated game is dissected and explored, with plenty of diagrams and a wealth of clarifying explanation. To reinforce certain key ideas, Oliver has inserted a range of questions. The answers to these numbered questions can be found in a section at the back of the book.

The icing on the cake is the threefold way the author concludes each game. He provides a summary of cardinal themes, encapsulates what he most remembers about the examined game, and closes with his favorite move. Although Oliver is only ten years old, his systematic presentation and the way he encompasses each lesson in a storytelling narrative evince a rare teaching mastery.

Now that I have digested and thoroughly appreciated each lesson, I can earnestly say I especially extol the book's pithy, intelligent commentary and its wide, educative value. I fully recommend it to all those wishing to improve their grasp of fundamentals. Aficionados will also enjoy it for fresh reinforcement and passionate overview. Young or old, new to the game or experienced, readers will find Oliver Boydell's first book to be a touchstone for challenge and inspiration.

Bruce Pandolfini

INTRODUCTION

I don't remember the exact moment I learned about chess. But I do remember instantly liking the game I saw in front of me with all the curious pieces.

My mother tells me that I taught myself how to play chess when I was five years old. I was mesmerized. And I just wanted to play as often as I could. I have many other interests (soccer, skiing, video games, the Rubik's Cube). But my favorite thing to do is play chess.

It didn't take long before I started playing in tournaments, and it was very exciting. I loved competition and the thrill of winning.

Soon, I was competing in big scholastic tournaments. I'm so happy that my mother supported my passion from the start. It's because of her that I was able to attend all the major scholastic events. I was in kindergarten when I played in my first Nationals. Working hard to develop my playing ability, I became a National Scholastic Champion in 2015. One year later, I played in the New York City Scholastic Championship and became New York City Champion.

I really enjoy talking about chess with others, both kids and adults. And going all the way back to my kindergarten homeroom, I also began teaching the game. Waiting for class to begin, I would give little lessons to my classmates on the finer points of chess. I think everyone should know not just how to play it, but how to play it well.

I've always loved this game and wanted to give others the chance to love it, too. That's how I ended up writing this book. I wanted to show how exciting a game chess can be!

To make this book happen, I compiled and analyzed some of the best chess games ever played. It wasn't easy to find them. And it was even harder to choose 25 games. I had to play through and review countless games from collections and databases. I learned so much from studying the greatest chess players who ever lived, especially Mikhail Botvinnik, Akiba Rubinstein, and Boris Spassky. I hope all of you experience their magic in these pages. They've got moves!

I've also learned tremendously from my private coaches Tomo Fukui, Pradeep Pathak, and Bruce Pandolfini. These super teachers and the outstanding champions mentioned above have taught me how to win. But they've also taught me something else: how to enjoy chess for the fantastic game it is. I'm very thankful to all those who accompanied and inspired me on my chess journey.

But most of all, I must thank my amazing and brilliant mother. Without her love, guidance, dedication, and many wonderful skills, I could never have written this book.

Oliver Boydell

GAME 1
THE IMMORTAL GAME

Adolf Anderssen vs. Lionel Kieseritzky, London 1851

King's Gambit Accepted

This is certainly among the best-known chess games. It was played while Adolf Anderssen (1818–1879) was winning the London 1851 tournament, the first international tournament ever. It is so famous that most people call it simply the Immortal Game. Anderssen sacrifices his queen and two rooks. But in the end, he only needs minor pieces to bring about an unforgettable mate.

1. e4   e5

2. f4
The King's Gambit. White plays to open the f-file and to draw away the e5-pawn.

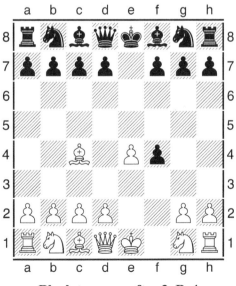

Black to move after 3. Bc4

2. ...exf4
The King's Gambit Accepted. The idea is that White can more easily play an eventual d2-d4.

3. Bc4
The Bishop's Gambit. White's bishop move doesn't stop a check at h4, as 3. Nf3 would.

3. ...Qh4+
So Black gives this check. White's king is pretty much forced to move. It's not safe to play 4. g3. But moving the White king turns out not to be important in the end.

4. Kf1   b5
A totally unnecessary gambit. That's the way they played in the 1850s.

5. Bxb5   Nf6
Pestering the e-pawn.

6. Nf3
White gains a tempo on the Black queen. Anderssen loves to attack.

6. ...Qh6
Black retreats the queen and keeps f4 guarded.

7. d3
Anderssen moves the d-pawn, but only one square. In this way, he protects e4.

7. ...Nh5

QUESTION 1: Why does Black play 7...Nh5?

8. Nh4
Closing the h-file and stopping 8...Ng3+.

8. ...Qg5
A double attack. Both the bishop on b5 and the knight on h4 are threatened.

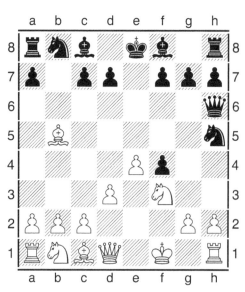

White to move after 7. ...Nh5

9. Nf5
The knight invades to an active post, momentarily saving both pieces.

9. ...c6
Attacking the bishop. Will it retreat to a4 or c4?

10. g4
Rather than defend, Anderssen prefers attack – always!

10. ...Nf6
Retreating the knight to safety.

11. Rg1
For tactical purposes, Anderssen lets his bishop go. He has bigger fish to fry.

11. ...cxb5
It's hard to turn down a free piece.

12. h4
Suddenly, things are getting uncomfortable for Black's queen.

12. ...Qg6
The only safe place for the Black queen.

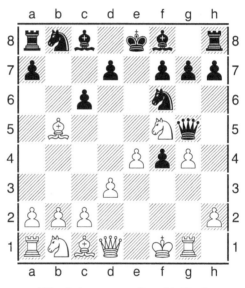

Black to move after 11. Rg1

13. h5   Qg5
Again, the only safe
square for the queen.

14. Qf3
White is threatening to
trap the Black queen by
Bc1xf4.

14. ...Ng8
This gives the queen a
diagonal escape.

15. Bxf4
Developing with a threat
to the queen.

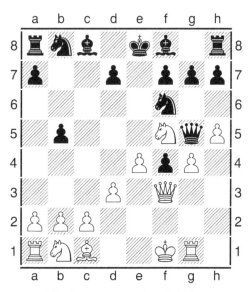

Black to move after 14. Qf3

15. ...Qf6
Attacking b2.

16. Nc3
Shielding b2.

16. ...Bc5
The g1-rook is threatened.

17. Nd5
The knight moves into
position. Attack, attack,
attack!

17. ...Qxb2
Both White rooks are now
threatened.

18. Bd6!
Anderssen appears to
ignore the threats.

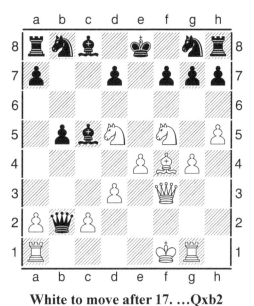

White to move after 17. ...Qxb2

18. ...Bxg1

One rook down, and the other is now hanging with check.

19. e5!

Perhaps the deepest move of the game. The Black queen is blocked out.

19. ...Qxa1+

20. Ke2   Na6

Black protects the c7-square.

21. Nxg7+

This works because the Black queen is no longer guarding g7.

21. ...Kd8

And now comes the finish.

22. Qf6+!   Nxf6

23. Be7 mate!

White didn't need his queen or rooks. His minor pieces do the job!

White wins (1-0)

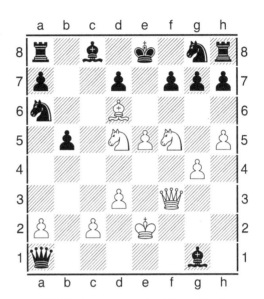

White to move after 20. ...Na6

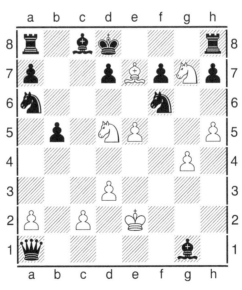

Black is mated after 23. Be7

I will always remember how Anderssen didn't need major pieces.

LESSONS LEARNED

* If you're going to attack, be prepared to use everything.

* You can move your king early and still be okay.

* Don't make showy sacrifices. Sacrifice only for good reasons.

My Favorite Move   22. Qf6+!

GAME 2
MY FAVORITE OPERA

Paul Morphy vs. the Allies, Paris 1858

The Philidor Defense

This might be the most famous chess game ever played. It was won by Paul Morphy (1837–1884). His opponents were a duke and a count working as a team. The game was played at the Paris Opera and it was a very quick game. It taught me valuable lessons, as it did the entire chess world.

1. e4   e5

2. Nf3   d6
The Philidor Defense, named after the great French master François-André Danican Philidor (1726–1795).

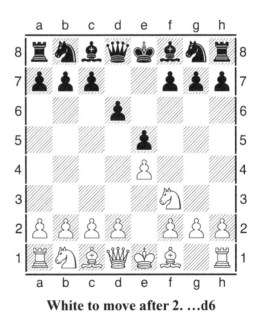

White to move after 2. …d6

3. d4   Bg4
This pin is premature.

4. dxe5   Bxf3
Black must take the knight. Otherwise, he loses a pawn.

QUESTION 2: What happens if 4…dxe5 instead?

5. Qxf3
This is the more natural recapture. It develops a piece and avoids doubled pawns.

5. ...dxe5
Black takes the pawn back.

6. Bc4
Developing with a threat.

6. ...Nf6
Defending by obstructing the queen.

7. Qb3!
Double attack: b7 and f7. White wins at least a pawn.

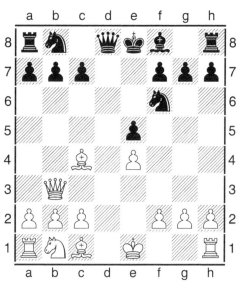

Black to move after 7. Qb3!

7. ...Qe7
This is an indirect defense of the a8-rook. If now 8. Qxb7, Black saves the rook by 8...Qb4+. That forces a queen trade. But he'd still be down a pawn.

8. Nc3
Morphy develops instead of taking a pawn. That was Morphy's great contribution: the principle of development.

8. ...c6
Black defends b7 directly with his queen.

9. Bg5
Pinning the f6-knight.

9. ...b5
Hoping to drive back the c4-bishop.

10. Nxb5!
Surprise!

10. ...cxb5

11. Bxb5+
This is better than taking with the queen. Why have the general do what can be done by the private?

11. ...Nbd7

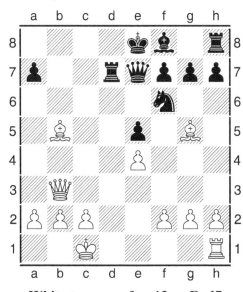

Black to move after 10. Nxb5!

12. 0–0–0
White castles queenside. He castles for attack, not for defense.

12. ...Rd8
Black adds protection to his d7-knight.

13. Rxd7!
White takes with the rook to keep the pin.

13. ...Rxd7

14. Rd1!
Piling up on the pinned rook.

14. ...Qe6
Unpinning his queen and offering a trade. If under attack, trading off some of the attackers is a good idea.

White to move after 13. ...Rxd7

15. Bxd7+
White had a couple of other winning ideas, but this one is more elegant.

15. ...Nxd7

16. Qb8+!!
A brilliant queen sacrifice! It forces open the d-file.

16. ...Nxb8
The only move.

17. Rd8 mate!
An incredible finish. It's often called Morphy's Mate, with the rook protected by the bishop. White used all his pieces. That's the power of development!

White wins (1-0)

I will always remember Morphy's queen sacrifice.

LESSONS LEARNED
* Develop all the pieces.
* Keep the initiative.
* Castling can be an attacking move.

My Favorite Move

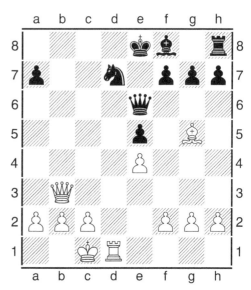

White to move after 15. ...Nxd7

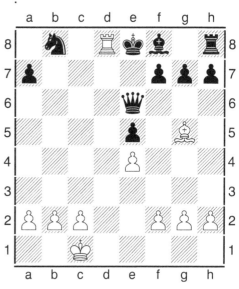

Black is mated after 17. Rd8

16. Qb8+!!

GAME 3
TRIPLING IS A HOMER

Siegbert Tarrasch vs. Isidor Gunsberg, Frankfurt 1887

The French Defense, Rubinstein Variation

It's very easy to understand the playing style of Dr. Siegbert Tarrasch (1862–1934). He liked open lines, straightforward development, centralization, two bishops, greater space and mobility, the initiative, and direct attacks against the opposing king. He loved to double and even triple major pieces before breaking through. The way he tripled in this game is almost unbelievable – but it worked!

1. e4   e6
The French Defense.

2. d4   d5

3. Nc3   dxe4
This capture gives us the Rubinstein Variation of the French Defense.

4. Nxe4
At this point, White has what's known as the "little center." A pawn on d4 vs. a pawn on e6. White has more space because his center pawn is further advanced than Black's.

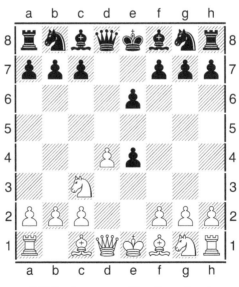

White to move after 3. …dxe4

4. ...Nf6
Immediately challenging White's knight.

5. Bd3
Also playable were 5. Bg5 or 5. Nxf6+.

5. ...Nbd7
One knight protects the other.

6. Be3   Nxe4

7. Bxe4   Nf6
Gaining a tempo, but it does not take away White's space edge.

8. Bd3   Bd7
Not the greatest bishop development.

9. Nf3   Bd6

10. 0-0   Ng4
Black goes after White's dark-square bishop.

11. Bg5
Tarrasch keeps his bishop. That's his style.

11. ...f6
Black gains a tempo, but he weakens the e6-pawn.

12. Bd2
The bishop is safe for now at d2. Tarrasch doesn't mind wasting a few moves to keep his bishop.

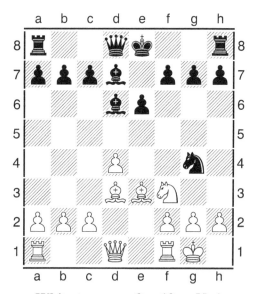

White to move after 10. ...Ng4

12. ...Qe7
Black readies queenside castling.

13. h3
Go away knight!

13. …Nh6

14. c4
Many players would
prefer taking the knight,
14. Bxh6 gxh6, busting up
Black's kingside pawns.
But not Tarrasch. He
prefers keeping the two
bishops.

14. …c6

<u>QUESTION 3</u>: How
would White have an-
swered 14…Nf7?

15. b4
Played in anticipation of
queenside castling.

15. …0-0-0
A risky move. But Black
didn't like kingside cas-
tling.

16. Re1   Bxb4
Black takes a doubtful
pawn.

17. Rb1
Now we see why Tarrasch
sacrificed the pawn. He
wanted to open the b-file
for attack.

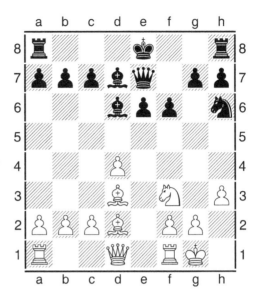

White to move after 13. …Nh6

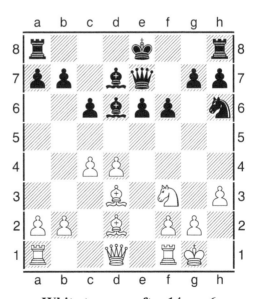

White to move after 14. …c6

17. ...Bxd2

18. Qxd2
Black has a pawn. White has the play.

18. ...Kb8
Hoping to get to a safer place.

19. c5
Shutting out the black queen and opening a diagonal for his bishop.

Black to move after 18. Qxd2

19. ...Bc8
This retreat adds two protectors to b7.

20. Rb3
It looks like White is starting to build his attack.

20. ...Qc7
Black was afraid White's queen would come to a5.

21. Reb1
Doubling rooks.

21. ...Ka8
Running to the corner for safety.

Black to move after 22. Rb6!

22. Rb6!
This blocks out Black's queen. Meanwhile, after 22...axb6 23. cxb6, Black must save his queen and stop 24. Qa5+. No way!

22. ...e5
Trying to open the d-file, to get tactical play against the white queen.

23. R1b4!
A rook lift, but to the 4th rank.

QUESTION 4: What follows after 23...axb6?

23. ...Rhe8
Black's development is good, but only superficially.

24. dxe5   fxe5

25. Ra4
Pinning the a-pawn.

25. ...e4
White's bishop is pinned, and his minor pieces are forked. But none of that is important.

26. Qa5!
The threat is mate.

26. ...Qb8
Black's position is very cramped.

27. Bxe4
Capturing the forking pawn.

27. ...Bf5

28. Ra6!!
White's major pieces are tripled in the most unex-

Black to move after 28. Ra6!!

pected way. Mate is threatened. If 28...bxa6, then 29. Bxc6+.

28. …Rd1+

29. Ne1   Rxe1+
Deflecting the White queen.

30. Qxe1   Bxe4

31. Rxe4   Rxe4

32. Qxe4   bxa6
The smoke has cleared.
Black has that extra
garbage knight, but his
position is about to fall
apart, thanks to White's
centralized queen.

33. Qxc6+   Qb7

34. Qe8+   Qb8

35. Qe4+
Once again, the queen is
centralized.

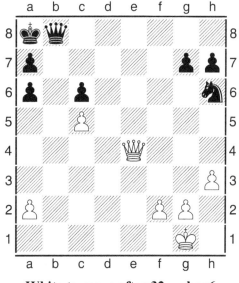

White to move after 32. …bxa6

35. …Qb7

36. c6!
In your face! White's centralized queen supports the pawn and
oversees the entire operation.

36. …Qc7
Trying to blockade the dangerous passed pawn.

37. Qe8+   Qb8

38. Qd7!   Qb1+

39. Kh2   Nf5

40. c7
There's no stopping promotion at c8. A classic performance!

Black resigns (1-0)

I will always remember how Tarrasch tripled his major pieces on the a-file.

LESSONS LEARNED

* The attacker needs open lines.

* Don't trade good pieces for bad.

Black to move after 40. c7

My Favorite Move   **22. Rb6!**

GAME 4
THE OLD LION

Wilhelm Steinitz vs. Curt von Bardeleben, Hastings 1895

Giuoco Piano

Wilhelm Steinitz (1836–1900) was 59 years old when he competed in the great Hastings tournament of 1895. He had just lost his world title to Emanuel Lasker (1868–1941) a year before. Most of the participants at the English event were much younger than Steinitz. One of the young competitors, Curt von Bardeleben (1861–1924), treated Steinitz a little rudely. But the feisty Steinitz got the last laugh.

1. e4   e5

2. Nf3   Nc6

3. Bc4   Bc5
The Giuoco Piano.

4. c3
White prepares to play d2-d4.

4. …Nf6
Attacking White's e-pawn.

5. d4
Advancing with threats.

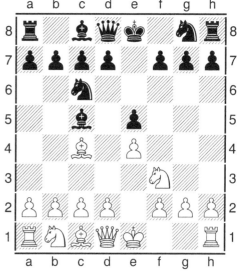

White to move after 3. …Bc5

5. ...exd4

6. cxd4
For the meantime, White has a classical pawn center.

6. ...Bb4+
Black needs this check to gain time.

7. Nc3
White could also have played 7. Bd2.

7. ...d5
Another way of playing is 7...Nxe4.

8. exd5   Nxd5
Black attacks c3 twice. It's defended only once.

9. 0–0
White gets his king out of the center. He hopes to use the e-file for attack.

9. ...Be6
Temporarily closing the e-file.

QUESTION 5: Does Black take the advantage after 9...Nxc3 10. bxc3 Bxc3?

10. Bg5
Attacking the queen.

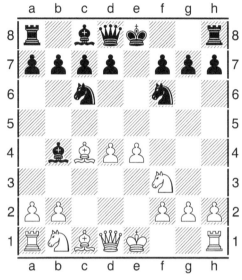

White to move after 6. ...Bb4+

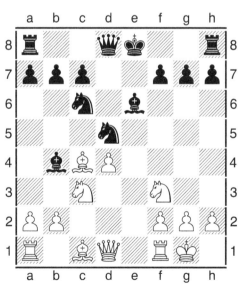

White to move after 9. ...Be6

35

10. ...Be7
White now trades a few pieces. He aims for pressure along the e-file.

11. Bxd5   Bxd5
The e-file is becoming more vulnerable for Black.

12. Nxd5   Qxd5

13. Bxe7   Nxe7

14. Re1!
This pin stops Black from castling.

14. ...f6
Black prevents White from using e5. He also gives his king a square at f7.

15. Qe2
White doubles on the e-file, threatening mate. He also prevents castling.

15. ...Qd7
Black had to defend e7.

16. Rac1
White develops his last piece. Rooks love open files.

16. ...c6
Black overprotects d5 and tries to make the c-pawn safer.

17. d5!
The old man makes a young sacrifice! His knight is headed to d4.

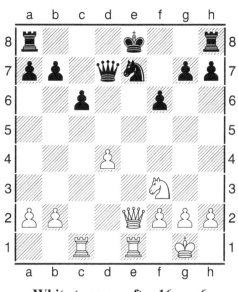

White to move after 16. ...c6

17. ...cxd5

18. Nd4
Now that the d4 square is unoccupied, White's knight makes good use of it.

18. ...Kf7
Black tries to use his king for defense. Maybe he can castle by hand.

19. Ne6
A menacing invasion.

19. ...Rhc8
With the king-rook in action, Black's king can maybe escape to the king-side.

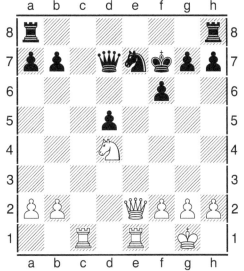

White to move after 18. ...Kf7

20. Qg4!
White has multiple threats.

20. ...g6
Protecting the g-pawn.

21. Ng5+
Black's queen is hanging.

21. ...Ke8
Protecting the queen.

22. Rxe7+!
Note that 22...Qxe7 is met by 23. Rxc8+.

22. ...Kf8
Black's queen can't be taken because of a back rank mate.

23. Rf7+   Kg8

24. Rg7+
White's rook is immune from capture.

24. ...Kh8
If White takes the black queen, Steinitz gets mated.

25. Rxh7+
Black technically resigned here. He simply walked out and let his clock forfeit. As soon as the flag fell, the wily Steinitz showed what he had in mind:

If 25...Kg8, then 26. Rg7+ Kh8 27. Qh4+ Kxg7 28. Qh7+ Kf8 29. Qh8+ Ke7 30. Qg7+ Ke8 31. Qg8+ Ke7 32. Qf7+ Kd8 33. Qf8+ Qe8 34. Nf7+ Kd7 35. Qd6 mate. A Swallow's Tail Mate!

Until the end of his life, Steinitz fought like a young lion.

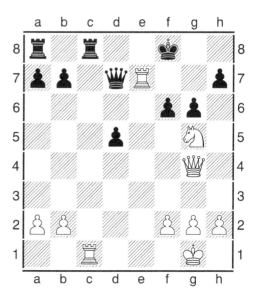

White to move after 22. ...Kf8

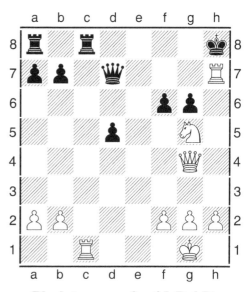

Black to move after 25. Rxh7+

Black resigns (1-0)

I will always remember how Steinitz blew the game open on the e-file.

LESSONS LEARNED

* Try to prevent your opponent from castling.

* Open lines for attack.

* Watch out for back rank mates.

<u>**My Favorite Move**</u>   17. d5!

GAME 5
THE SUPERIOR ROOK

Akiba Rubinstein vs. Emanuel Lasker, St. Petersburg 1909

Queen's Gambit Declined

Akiba Rubinstein (1882–1961) was perhaps the best endgame player. Many of his endgames are described in textbooks. He especially knew how to gain small advantages. He also had precise technique. In the following game, we see him outplaying another great endgame master, Emanuel Lasker.

1. d4   d5

2. Nf3   Nf6

3. c4   e6
The Queen's Gambit Declined.

4. Bg5   c5
The Tarrasch Defense.

5. cxd5   exd5

6. Nc3   cxd4
Lasker accepts an isolated d-pawn.

7. Nxd4   Nc6

8. e3
Defending the knight and letting out the king-bishop.

8. ...Be7

A quiet development.

9. Bb5   Bd7

Breaking the pin.

10. Bxf6

Removing a protector of d5.

10. ...Bxf6

11. Nxd5   Bxd4

12. exd4   Qg5

Black has dangerous
counterplay. The queen
attacks g2 and skewers
two minor pieces on the
White 5th rank.

13. Bxc6   Bxc6

14. Ne3

For the moment, White's
g-pawn is safe.

14. ...0–0–0

15. 0–0   Rhe8

Black threatens to take
the knight.

White to move after 12. ...Qg5

16. Rc1!

Rubinstein executes a clever defense.

16. ...Rxe3

QUESTION 6:
Can White safely take the rook?

17. Rxc6+! bxc6

18. Qc1!!
The White queen pins the rook on e3.

18. ...Rxd4

19. fxe3 Rd7
Black decides to defend his 2nd rank.

20. Qxc6+ Kd8

21. Rf4! f5

22. Qc5 Qe7
Lasker thinks he's okay in this endgame.

23. Qxe7+ Kxe7

24. Rxf5 Rd1+

25. Kf2!
Rubinstein knows he must activate his king, even if he loses a pawn.

25. ...Rd2+
Pigging out.

26. Kf3 Rxb2

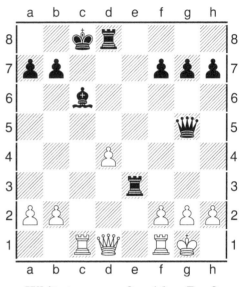

White to move after 16. ...Rxe3

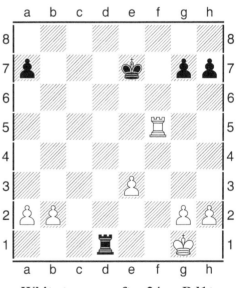

White to move after 24. ...Rd1+

42

27. Ra5!
A nice rook placement. It defends and attacks at the same time.

27. ...Rb7
Lasker thinks he's safe.

28. Ra6!
The rook cuts off the Black king.

28. ...Kf8

29. e4   Rc7
Black is playing for a draw.

30. h4!
White plans to move up his kingside pawns, supported by his king.

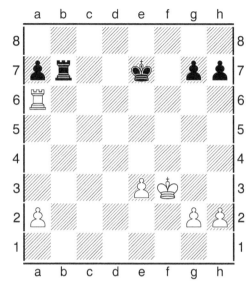

Black to move after 28. Ra6!

30. ...Kf7

31. g4   Kf8

32. Kf4   Ke7

33. h5!
Trying to force weaknesses on Black's kingside.

33. ...h6
This weakens g6.

34. Kf5   Kf7

35. e5
White has gradually moved up his forces.

35. ...Rb7

36. Rd6   Ke7
Preventing the sac Rd7+.

37. Ra6   Kf7

38. Rd6   Kf8

39. Rc6
Rubinstein knows he will have additional time for analysis at move 40, so he's not taking any chances.

39. ...Kf7

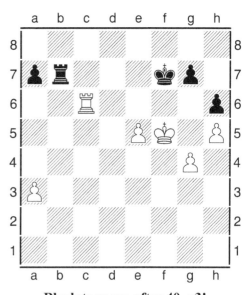

White to move after 35. ...Rb7

40. a3!
A very crafty move. It prevents the Black rook from going to b4. If 40...Kf8 or 40...Ke7, White has 41. Kg6. If 40...Re7, then 41. e6+ Kg8 42. Kg6 Re8 43. e7! will win. A masterful performance by Rubinstein.

Black resigns (1-0)

Black to move after 40. a3!

I will always remember how Rubinstein's king and pawns gradually moved up the board.

LESSONS LEARNED

* In the endgame, use your king.

* Rooks should create cutoffs.

* Look for indirect defenses.

<u>**My Favorite Move**</u>   **25. Kf2!**

GAME 6
GOING FOR THE GOLD

Stepan Levitsky vs. Frank Marshall, Breslau 1912

Queen's Gambit Declined

The story is part of chess lore. Frank Marshall (1877–1944) was a great crowd pleaser. It seemed he often played spectacular combinations to amaze an audience. The onlookers to our next game were startled. In fact, they were so shocked, as the story goes, that they threw gold pieces at the board. True or not, Marshall's final move was indeed brilliant.

1. e4   e6
The French Defense.

2. d4   d5

3. Nc3
Developing the knight.

3. ...c5
The Tarrasch Variation. There is a good chance Black will have to accept an isolated d-pawn.

4. Nf3
Developing and defending the center.

4. ...Nc6
Increasing pressure against the center.

5. exd5   exd5
It's likely that Black will have to accept an isolated d-pawn.

6. Be2
Closing the e-file temporarily. White is ready to castle.

6. ...Nf6

7. 0–0   Be7
Black, in turn, is set up to castle.

8. Bg5
White's dark-square bishop attacks dark squares directly and light squares indirectly. By eventually taking the knight, the light squares d5 and e4 will be weakened.

8. ...0–0

9. dxc5
Sure enough, Black's d-pawn is now isolated. But he does get open lines for attack.

9. ...Be6
Marshall makes sure his d-pawn is supported before taking back on c5.

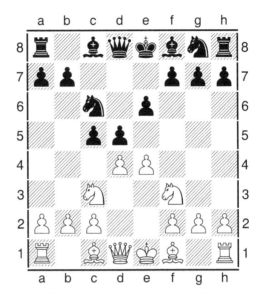
White to move after 4. ...Nc6

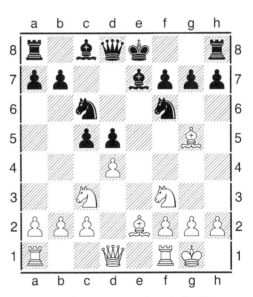
Black to move after 8. Bg5

10. Nd4
Occupying the square in front of the isolated d-pawn.

10. ...Bxc5

11. Nxe6
White plays for the two bishops.

11. ...fxe6
Black gets an open line for the f8-rook, and his d-pawn is no longer isolated. But his e-pawn is now a potential target.

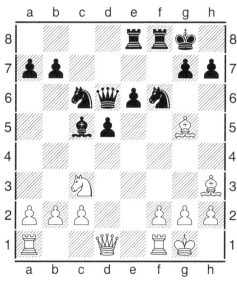

Black to move after 11. Nxe6

12. Bg4
White goes right after it.

12. ...Qd6
Marshall defends his e-pawn. He also connects his rooks.

13. Bh3
White gets his bishop to safety.

13. ...Rae8
Marshall develops his last piece.

14. Qd2
Connecting his own rooks. But the White queen is not well placed on d2.

White to move after 13. ...Rae8

14. ...Bb4

Pinning the knight, with threats. I told you the queen might be in trouble on d2.

15. Bxf6

White was afraid of Nf6-e4.

15. ...Rxf6

16. Rad1   Qc5

Black is starting to create some pressure. He might advance the d-pawn.

17. Qe2

Getting out of the diagonal pin.

17. ...Bxc3

18. bxc3   Qxc3

Marshall wins a pawn. Or does he?

19. Rxd5

The pin on the e-pawn allows this capture.

19. ...Nd4!

But now it starts to get tricky.

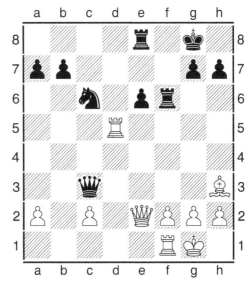

White to move after 16. ...Qc5

Black to move after 19. Rxd5

49

20. Qh5?

Attacking the rook at e8 – but not the best move. 20. Qe4 would have been better, centralizing and keeping the pin.

20. ...Ref8
Doubling rooks on the f-file.

21. Re5
Moving the rook to safety.

21. ...Rh6
The White queen is attacked.

22. Qg5
Putting the queen on a forkable square.

22. ...Rxh3!
If 23. gxh3, then 23… Nf3+ wins.

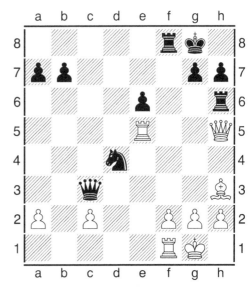

White to move after 21. ...Rh6

23. Rc5
Counterattacking the Black queen.

23. ...Qg3!!
An incredible finishing move!

White resigns (0–1)

QUESTION 7: Why can't White simply take the Black queen?

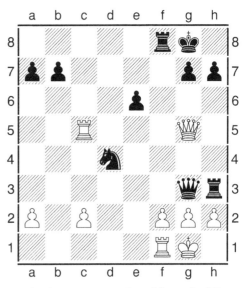

White to move after 23. ...Qg3!!

I will always remember how Marshall put his queen where two pawns could take it.

LESSONS LEARNED

* When you control open lines, use them for attack.

* Just because a move looks good doesn't mean it is.

* Don't put your pieces in pins.

My Favorite Move   23. …Qg3!!

GAME 7
THE CZAR'S GRANDMASTERS

Emanuel Lasker vs. Jose Capablanca, St. Petersburg 1914

Ruy Lopez, Exchange Variation

Jose Capablanca (1888–1942) needed to draw the following game to pretty much lock up first prize. But it's not always easy to draw when you need one. True or not, the Czar of Russia supposedly designated the top five placers in this event as Grandmasters. Thus, according to legend, Emanuel Lasker, Jose Capablanca, Alexander Alekhine (1892–1946), Siegbert Tarrasch, and Frank Marshall became the first five Grandmasters.

1. e4	**e5**
2. Nf3	**Nc6**
3. Bb5	**a6**

The Morphy Defense.

4. Bxc6
The Exchange Variation.

4. ...dxc6
Taking away from the center (instead of toward it) for tactical reasons.

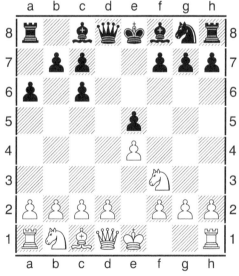

White to move after 4. ...dxc6

5. d4
Trying to create a kingside pawn majority.

5. ...exd4

6. Qxd4

QUESTION 8: Why does White play 6. Qxd4 instead of 6. Nxd4?

6. ...Qxd4

7. Nxd4
White has a kingside pawn majority, and Black has a queenside majority. But Black's majority is messed up.

7. ...Bd6
Developing and defending the c7-pawn.

8. Nc3   Ne7
The knight is safer at e7 than f6.

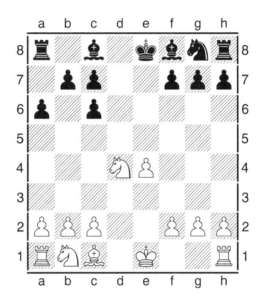

Black to move after 7. Nxd4

9. 0–0   0–0
Both sides are ready for business.

10. f4
Capablanca's Rule says that when advancing a pawn majority, you should move the unopposed pawn first. Let's see how Lasker continues.

10. ...Re8
Aiming at White's e4-pawn and trying to discourage e4-e5.

11. Nb3
This safeguards against a pin along the a7-g1 diagonal.

11. ...f6
Making it tougher for White to advance his king-pawn.

12. f5!
Lasker violates Capablanca's Rule! You might say he has a plan.

12. ...b6
Capablanca wants to flank his queen-bishop. But the bishop is better placed if it guards e6.

13. Bf4!
What? Is Lasker now threatening to help Capablanca out by undoubling his pawns?

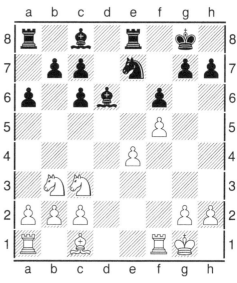

Black to move after 12. f5!

13. ...Bb7
It turns out that 13...Bxf4 was better for Black.

14. Bxd6!
Yes! Lasker undoubles the black c-pawns! Why? Because it's easier to attack the healthy pawn at d6 than it is to attack the doubled pawn at c7.

14. ...cxd6
Black has healthier pawns, but a weaker position. Go figure.

15. Nd4
The knight is headed for e6.

15. ...Rad8?
15...Bc8 would have been better.

16. Ne6
What a great knight. A monster knight!

16. ...Rd7

17. Rad1
Aiming at the d6-pawn.

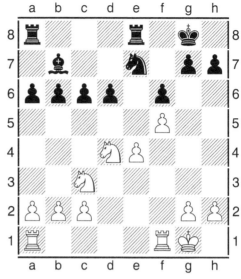

Black to move after 15. Nd4

17. ...Nc8
Black is playing so defensively. Capablanca seems intimidated.

18. Rf2
Preparing to double on the d-file.

18. ...b5
Trying to gain queenside space, as well as clearing b6 for the knight.

19. Rfd2
This discourages the Black knight from moving anywhere.

19. ...Rde7
The Black rook gets off the d-file.

20. b4
Holding back Black's
b-pawn.

20. ...Kf7
Capablanca expects ac-
tion on the g-file, sooner
or later. So he moves the
king to the f-file.

21. a3
Guarding b4, so he
doesn't have to think
about defending it later.

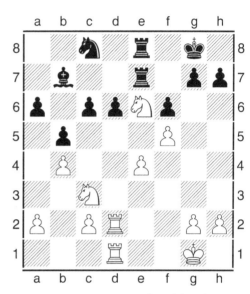

Black to move after 20. b4

21. ...Ba8?
Black is trying to get play
by opening the a-file. This
turns against him.

22. Kf2
Each side activates the king for the endgame.

22. ...Ra7
Preparing to advance the a-pawn.

23. g4
Activity on the g-file proceeds.

23. ...h6
To stop g4-g5.

24. Rd3
Now the rook can shift along the 3rd rank.

24. ...a5

25. h4
Supporting an upcoming g4-g5.

25. ...axb4

26. axb4   Rae7
Black decides he can't really use the a-file profitably.

27. Kf3
Moving up the king. But White must be careful of potential dangers along the a8-h1 diagonal.

27. ...Rg8
Black would love to open the g-file to his favor.

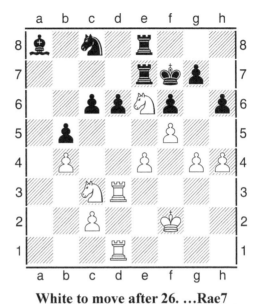

White to move after 26. ...Rae7

28. Kf4
In the tradition of Steinitz, Lasker always tries to get an active king's position.

28. ...g6

29. Rg3   g5+

30. Kf3
If 30...gxh4, White gets the h-file after 31. Rh3.

30. ...Nb6
Now it is White who will gain the h-file.

31. hxg5   hxg5

32. Rh3!
Sure enough, White gets control of the h-file.

Black to move after 30. Kf3

32. ...Rd7
Th d-pawn had to be defended.

33. Kg3
An important setup move. White gets his king off the a8-h1 diagonal.

33. ...Ke8
Black's king is starting to get in the way of his rooks.

34. Rdh1
Doubling on the h-file.

34. ...Bb7

35. e5!
A clearance sacrifice!
Clearing the e4-square.

35. ...dxe5

36. Ne4
Devastating.

36. ...Nd5
This doesn't work.

37. N6c5
Winning the Exchange.

37. ...Bc8

38. Nxd7   Bxd7

39. Rh7!
Seizing the 7th rank.

39. ...Rf8

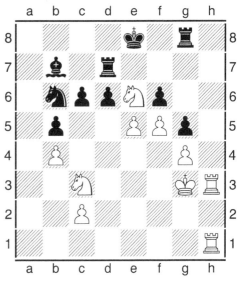

Black to move after 35. e5!

40. Ra1!
Shifting flanks, taking the a-file. Black's plan has backfired.

40. ...Kd8

41. Ra8+   Bc8

42. Nc5
It's hopeless. White is threatening several different mates. What a masterpiece!

Black resigns (1–0)

I will always remember how Lasker undoubled Capablanca's c-pawns.

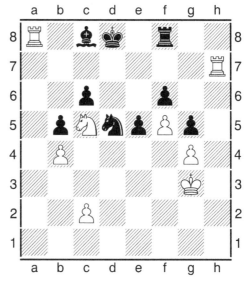

Black to move after 42. Nc5

<u>LESSONS LEARNED</u>

* Doubled pawns can be stronger than undoubled ones.

* Try to create favorable pawn majorities.

* Get your rooks to open files and then to the 7th rank.

<u>My Favorite Move</u>   35. e5!

GAME 8
FLANK TO FLANK

David Janowski vs. Jose Capablanca, New York 1916

The Liberated Bishop's Defense

Jose Capablanca was one of the greatest players. He learned at the age of four, with an intuitive feel for positions. But he was a little lazy. Sometimes he played the opening carelessly. He would get into trouble and have to use his genius to save himself. That's pretty much what he does in the following game against his friend David Janowski (1868–1927).

1. d4   Nf6

2. Nf3   d5
A double queen pawn game by transposition.

3. c4   c6
This is a kind of Slav Defense.

4. Nc3   Bf5
Now it has become a modern Liberated Bishop's Defense. There's a problem here. When the Black queen-bishop is developed too early, the b7-pawn can become a target.

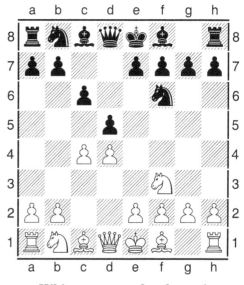

White to move after 3. ….c6

5. Qb3
It's better to play 5. cxd5 cxd5 and then 6. Qb3.

5. ...Qb6
Black offers a queen trade.

6. Qxb6
White plays to create double isolated b-pawns.

6. ...axb6
One positive for Black is that he opens the a-file for his rook.

7. cxd5   Nxd5
Trying to avoid any further pawn weaknesses.

8. Nxd5   cxd5
But it couldn't be helped. Black has doubled isolated b-pawns.

9. e3
Capablanca is saddled with pawn weaknesses. How is he going to survive?

9. ...Nc6
Black has a slight lead in development. White must worry about the knight invading at b4.

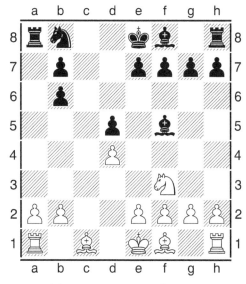

White to move after 8. ...cxd5

10. Bd2
White guards b4.

10. ...Bd7!
Capablanca admits his mistake. He makes sure not to play 10...e6, since that would lock the bishop outside the pawn chain. He wants it inside the pawn chain! Why? Because he has a plan.

11. Be2
A quiet but steady development.

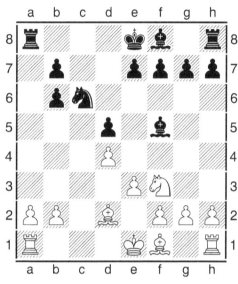

Black to move after 10. Bd2

11. ...e6
Now the king-bishop can come out.

12. 0-0   Bd6
A good centralization.

13. Rfc1
White now has a rook on an open file.

13. ...Ke7!
Another breaking of principle! Capablanca realizes there's no need to castle. Better to keep the king in the center for the upcoming endgame.

14. Bc3   Rhc8
Black has weakened pawns, but he has open lines for compensation.

15. a3
Weakening the queenside light squares.

15. ...Na5
Heading for those weak squares.

16. Nd2
Trying to guard those weakened light squares.

16. …f5
Capablanca plays to restrain the advance e3-e4.

17. g3
This is played to stop f5-f4.

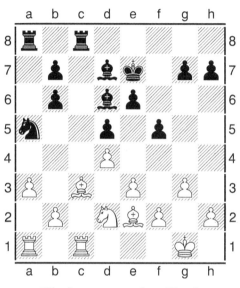

Black to move after 17. g3

17. …b5
Thanks to the bishop being at d7, Black now has support for this advance.

18. f3
Hoping to reinforce the e3-e4 advance.

18. …Nc4
The knight is supported nicely by the isolated b5-pawn.

19. Bxc4   bxc4
Capablanca has gotten rid of his pawn weakness. Moreover, he also has the two bishops.

20. e4   Kf7
Getting off the e-file.

21. e5   Be7
Capablanca keeps the bishop located centrally, so he can attack on both the kingside and the queenside.

22. f4
Don't look now – but every White pawn is on a dark square.

22. ...b5
Queenside mobilization continues.

23. Kf2
White activates his king for the endgame. In the endgame, as long as they are safe, kings like to be in the center.

23. ...Ra4
Black's pressure mounts.

24. Ke3   Rca8
The rooks are doubled on the a-file. The threat is b5-b4.

25. Rab1
White gets out of the a-file pin.

25. ...h6
Beautiful! With the focus being on the queenside, Capablanca suddenly shifts attention to the kingside!

26. Nf3   g5
It's so elegant how Capablanca has managed his pawns.

Black to move after 22. f4

White to move after 24. ...Rca8

27. Ne1 Rg8
Time to bring in reinforcements.

28. Kf3 gxf4

29. gxf4

QUESTION 9: What happens on 29. Kxf4?

29. ...Raa8
The rook gets ready to shift over to the kingside. Capablanca is playing a two-flank game. White isn't as flexible. His knight is in the way of his rooks

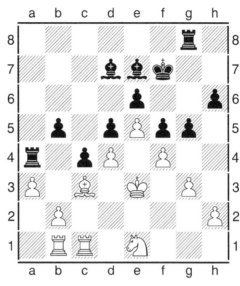

White to move after 27. ...Rg8

30. Ng2 Rg4

31. Rg1 Rag8
Now Black has doubled rooks on the g-file!

32. Be1
White's pieces lack coordination. They're getting in each other's way.

32. ...b4!
A creative pawn sacrifice with a purpose.

33. axb4 Ba4!
Now the bishop has a way to head toward e4, a powerfully centralized square.

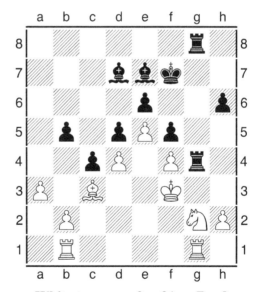

White to move after 31. ...Rag8

34. Ra1
White tries to generate some rook activity.

34. ...Bc2

35. Bg3
Hoping to relieve the g-file pin.

35. ...Be4+
A tremendous centralization.

36. Kf2   h5
This pawn is getting ready for further advance.

37. Ra7
Taking the 7th rank.

37. ...Bxg2
It is amazing how this bishop has become such a weapon. Black will now exploit the g-file pin.

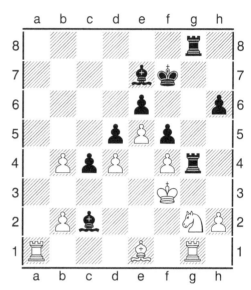

White to move after 34. ...Bc2

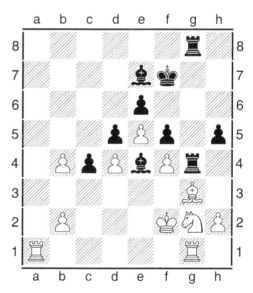

White to move after 36. ...h5

38. Rxg2   h4
This wins the Exchange.

39. Bxh4   Rxg2+

40. Kf3   Rxh2
Gobble gobble.

41. Bxe7   Rh3+

42. Kf2   Rb3
Shifting from the kingside back to the queenside!

43. Bg5+   Kg6

44. Re7   Rxb2+

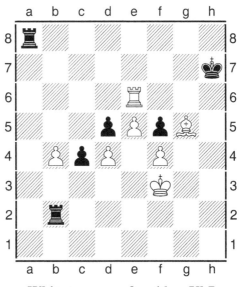

White to move after 38. …h4

45. Kf3   Ra8!
And now the other rook shifts flanks. The threat is mate.

46. Rxe6+   Kh7
It's hopeless. If White tries to make a run for it with 47. Kg3, there follows 47…Ra3+ 48. Kh4 Rh2 mate!

White resigns (0-1)

White to move after 46. …Kh7

I will always remember how Capablanca retreated his bishop inside the pawn chain.

LESSONS LEARNED

* If you have isolated pawns, try to trade them off.

* Don't develop the queen-bishop too early.

* In blocked positions, try to get play on both flanks.

My Favorite Move   **10. ...Bd7!**

GAME 9
CORNERED!

Aron Nimzowitsch vs. Arthur Hakansson, Kristianstad 1922

The French Defense

Aron Nimzowitsch (1886–1935) was one of the most important chess thinkers. He reacted strongly against the principles in the way they were stated by Tarrasch. In his landmark book, *My System*, Nimzowitsch put forth new principles. These ideas have greatly influenced chess ever since. Consider his game against Arthur Hakansson (1889–1947). In it, we see Black restricted and cramped into a surprising checkmate.

1. e4   e6
The French Defense.

2. d4   d5

3. e5
The Advance Variation
of the French Defense.
White immediately closes
the center.

3. ...c5
Black attacks at the base
of the pawn chain. That's a
Nimzowitschean concept.

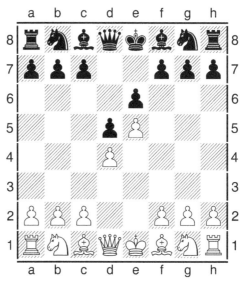

Black to move after 3. e5

4. Qg4
An idea popularized by Nimzowitsch. White tries to restrict the development of Black's king-bishop.

4. ...cxd4
Black destroys the base of White's pawn chain. He is temporarily up a pawn.

5. Nf3
Nimzowitsch's plan is to overprotect the e5-pawn. That will keep Black cramped.

5. ...Nc6

6. Bd3
Steady development.

6. ...f5
Black hopes White will capture *en passant*. Nimzowitsch has no intention of doing that.

7. Qg3
Still keeping the pressure on g7.

7. ...Nge7

8. 0-0   Ng6
Black is trying to shield g7 so he can develop the king-bishop.

9. h4
Preparing to drive away the g6-knight.

9. ...Qc7
Black attacks e5 and defends g7.

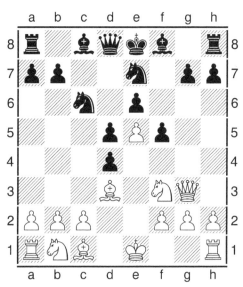

White to move after 7. ...Nge7

10. Re1
Once again, White secures his king-pawn, so that Black remains cramped.

10. ...Bd7?

QUESTION 10: What does 10...Bd7 suggest about Black's castling plans?

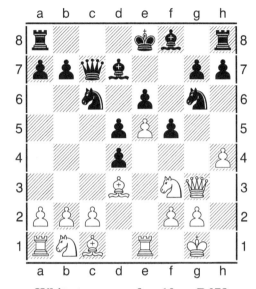

White to move after 10. ...Bd7?

11. a3
Expecting Black to castle queenside, White begins queenside activity.

11. ...0-0-0
Black does castle queenside.

12. b4
White gets the queenside pawns going.

12. ...a6
To stop an advancing pawn attack.

13. h5
Driving the knight back. White is playing on both flanks. This is easier to do when the center is closed, as it is here.

13. ...Nge7

14. Bd2
White gets ready to open the c-file.

14. ...h6?
Weakening g6.

15. a4
Here come the guys!

15. ...g5
Still hoping for White to take the pawn *en passant*, 16. hxg6, when 16...Rg8 gives Black activity.

16. b5   f4
An in-between move (a *zwischenzug*).

17. Qg4
Nimzowitsch's comment is memorable: "The queen is well placed here."

Black to move after 15. a4

17. ...Nb8
The knight goes back to its cubby hole.

18. c3
The c-file is going to be opened against the Black king.

18. ...Re8
Trying to give the Black king an escape square.

19. cxd4   Kd8
The king must get off the c-file.

Black to move after 17. Qg4

20. Rc1
White's rook takes control of the c-file.

20. ...Qb6

The queen will now be driven into a dungeon.

21. a5   Qa7

22. b6!   Qa8

This position is almost
funny – although it
probably wasn't funny to
Black.

23. Rc7

Nimzowitsch referred
to this as "The 7th Rank
Absolute." But for many of
us, White is just pigging
out.

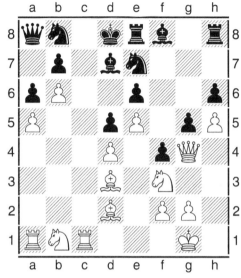

White to move after 22. ...Qa8

23. ...Nf5

Striving for freedom for
some counterplay.

24. Nc3

Nimzowitsch finally clears his home rank. He also has a threat.

24. ...Be7

25. Nxd5

Now if 25...exd5, then 26. Bxf5.

25. ...Nxd4

Black plays a desperado, hoping to avoid losing a pawn.

26. Nxd4   exd5
Now comes the final surprise.

27. Qxd7+!
Yes, the queen was well placed on g4!

Now if 27...Nxd7, then 28. Ne6 is mate. Black is smothered to death.

Black resigns (1-0)

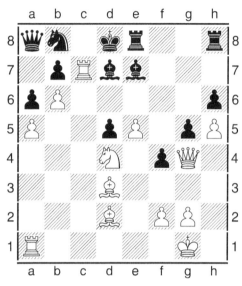

White to move after 26. ...exd5

I will always remember how Nimzowitsch drove Black's queen to the corner.

LESSONS LEARNED
* If the opponent is cramped, don't allow freeing trades.

* In closed centers, attack at the base of the pawn chain.

* Try to castle on the correct side.

My Favorite Move

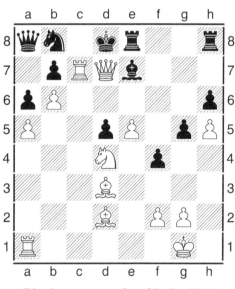

Black to move after 27. Qxd7+!

22. b6!

GAME 10
NIMZOWITSCH IS ZUGZWANGED

Alexander Alekhine vs. Aron Nimzowitsch, San Remo 1930

The French Defense, Winawer Variation

By 1930, after defeating Capablanca for the world championship in 1927, Alexander Alekhine was at the height of his creative powers. With a score of 14-1 at San Remo, Alekhine achieved one of the greatest ever triumphs of any chess player. Poor Nimzowitsch. He was a brilliant strategist and theoretician. But in the following game, Alekhine treats him like an amateur. Nimzo gets *zugzwanged!*

1. e4   e6
The French Defense.

2. d4   d5

3. Nc3   Bb4
The Winawer Variation. Black is attacking e4.

4. e5
Saving the e-pawn and gaining space.

4. ...c5

5. Bd2
A less expected move, but Alekhine could do anything at times. It does avoid doubled pawns.

5. ...Ne7

6. Nb5
Aiming to get in at d6.

6. ...Bxd2+

7. Qxd2   0–0

8. c3
Using Nimzowitsch
against Nimzowitsch.
Alekhine supports the
base of his pawn chain.

8. ...b6?
Weakening the queenside
light squares.

9. f4
Reinforcing e5.

9. ...Ba6
Naturally, Black tries to get some activity for this bishop.

10. Nf3   Qd7

11. a4!
Alekhine keeps the queenside under his control.

11. ...Nbc6

White to move after 5. ...Ne7

12. b4!
White gains space on the queenside.

12. ...cxb4

13. cxb4   Bb7
Nimzowitsch safeguards against a future pawn fork at b5.

14. Nd6
Invading on a wonderful outpost square.

14. ...f5
This is played to stop an eventual f4-f5 by White.

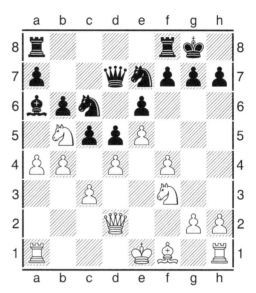

Black to move after 12. b4!

15. a5!
Black is getting extremely cramped.

15. ...Nc8
Black's pieces have limited scope.

16. Nxb7
Alekhine trades the good knight for the bad bishop! But this improves his grip on the light squares.

16. ...Qxb7

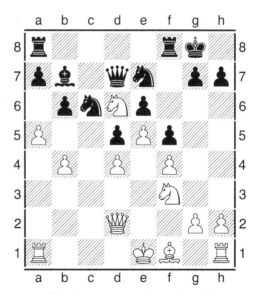

Black to move after 15. a5!

17. a6!
Take that queen!

If 17...Qe7 18. Bb5, can Black safely play 18...
Nxb4?

17. ...Qf7

18. Bb5!
White's bishop is very
strong.

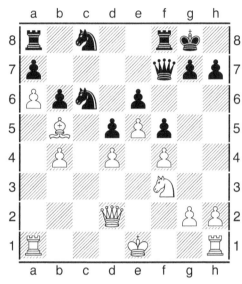

Black to move after 18. Bb5!

18. ...N8e7
The knights defend each
other. What's more, the
rooks are connected.

19. 0–0
In closed positions, one
can castle later – even
much later.

19. ...h6
Black wants to stop Ng5.

20. Rfc1
Rooks belong on open files.

20. ...Rfc8

21. Rc2
Alekhine prepares to double rooks.

21. ...Qe8

22. Rac1
In his notes, Alekhine found a better move. After 22. Ra3! Rc7 23.
Rac3 Rac8 24. Qc1, he has tripled major pieces on the c-file.

22. ...Rab8
In case of 23. Ba4, Nimzo hopes to play 23...b5.

23. Qe3 Rc7

24. Rc3
Alekhine has found another way to triple!

24. ...Qd7

25. R1c2 Kf8
Black thinks he may need
his king for defense on
the queenside.

26. Qc1!
Major pieces are tripled
on the c-file.

26. ...Rbc8

27. Ba4!
Threatening b4-b5.

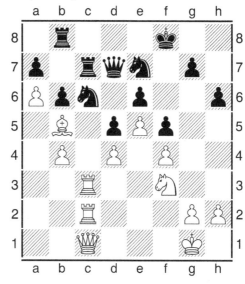

Black to move after 26. Qc1!

27. ...b5
So Black is forced to give up a pawn to gain defensive time.

28. Bxb5 Ke8
The black king is trying to get over to the queenside to shore up
defenses.

29. Ba4 Kd8
Now everything seems upheld.

30. h4!
But there's another problem. Black is in *zugzwang*!

30. ...Qe8
The square c7 is now weakened.

31. b5
And this wins material. "Constriction" is a Nimzowitschean concept. When you constrict a piece, you reduce its scope. In the end, look how constricted Black's own pieces are. They're on central files, but with no mobility.

Black resigns (1–0)

I will always remember how Alekhine tripled major pieces.

LESSONS LEARNED
* Trade good pieces for bad ones – but only if it gains advantage.

* In closed positions, keep your opponent constricted.

* Try to triple major pieces for greater control.

My Favorite Move

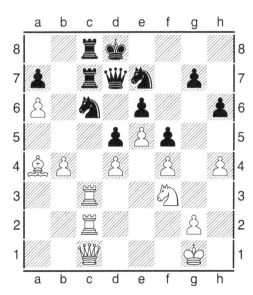

Black to move after 30. h4!

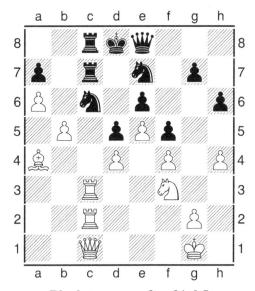

Black to move after 31. b5

30. h4!

GAME 11
ALEKHINE AT HIS BEST

Alexander Alekhine vs. Emanuel Lasker, Zurich 1934

Queen's Gambit Declined

How do you know you control more space? Sometimes your center pawns are further advanced. That gives you more room behind the lines. Sometimes you simply control more territory than your opponent. In this game, starting with a slight space advantage, Alekhine builds it into an unstoppable kingside attack. His unfortunate opponent? The great Lasker.

1. d4   d5

2. c4   e6
The Queen's Gambit Declined.

3. Nc3
Attacking d5 and e4.

3. ...Nf6
Fighting for the same squares as White.

4. Nf3   Be7

5. Bg5
Indirectly attacking d5 and e4.

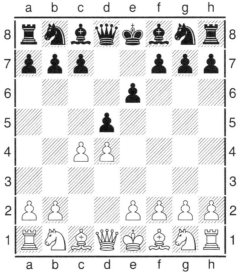

White to move after 2. ...e6

5. ...Nbd7
These moves are standard.

6. e3
Clearing the f1-bishop's diagonal.

6. ...0–0

7. Rc1
The rook is ready in case the c-file opens.

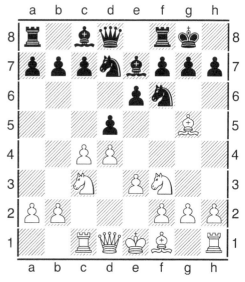

Black to move after 7. Rc1

7. ...c6
For now, Black has a strongpoint at d5.

8. Bd3
Alekhine knows he will have to move this bishop again.

8. ...dxc4
Forcing White to move the king-bishop a second time.

9. Bxc4   Nd5
Hoping to get an easier position by trading a few pieces.

10. Bxe7   Qxe7

11. Ne4
Alekhine liked to avoid trading his knight by shifting it toward the kingside.

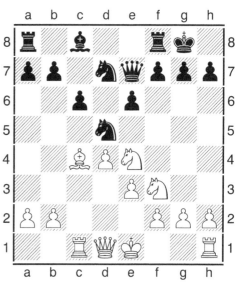

Black to move after 11. Ne4

11. ...N5f6
Still aiming for a trade.

12. Ng3   e5
Lasker naturally tries to free up the c8-bishop. The move does weaken f5, however.

13. 0–0   exd4

14. Nf5
White plans to take back on d4 with a knight.

14. ...Qd8

15. N3xd4
The center is open. Pieces can move through it.

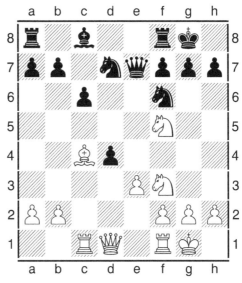

Black to move after 14. Nf5

15. ...Ne5
Attacking the bishop at c4.

16. Bb3   Bxf5
A minor victory for Black. Lasker trades off the "bad bishop."

17. Nxf5   Qb6?
This is a mistake. It removes the queen from the action. Alekhine capitalizes on the mistake at once.

18. Qd6!
A powerful invasion.

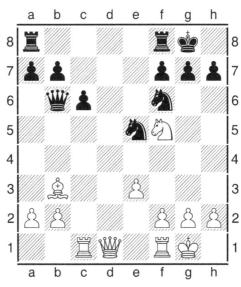

White to move after 17. ...Qb6?

18. …Ned7

QUESTION 12: What happens after 18…Ng6?

19. Rfd1
Alekhine's slight space edge now becomes huge.

19. …Rad8
Defending d7.

20. Qg3!
Alekhine uses the center to shift to a kingside attack.

20. ...g6
Black is forced to weaken his king's position.

21. Qg5
Increasing the pressure on the weakened dark squares.

21. …Kh8
Unpinning the g-pawn.

22. Nd6
For the second time this game, White exploits the weak d6 square.

22. …Kg7
To guard f7.

23. e4!
This move has two points. The advancing pawn becomes a weapon, and now the 3rd rank is clear for a rook lift.

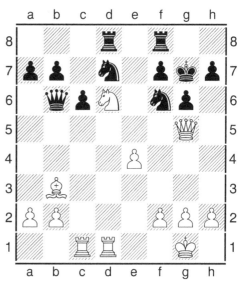

Black to move after 23. e4!

23. ...Ng8
Retreating to guard f6 and h6.

24. Rd3
A rook lift!

24. ...f6
Black is now lost. However, 24...h6 25. Nf5+ Kh7 26. Nxh6! Nxh6 27. Rh3 was also bad.

25. Nf5+   Kh8
Two White pieces are hanging.

26. Qxg6!!
Now, only one of them hangs. Lasker's goose is cooked. If 26...hxg6, then 27. Rh3+ mates.

Black resigns (1–0)

I will always remember how Alekhine shifted his attack from the center to the kingside.

LESSONS LEARNED

* Use the center to transfer to the kingside.

* Avoid weaknesses around your king.

My Favorite Move

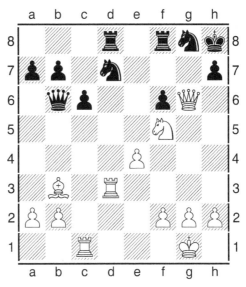

Black to move after 26. Qxg6!!

26. Qxg6!!

GAME 12
BOTVINNIK THE STRATEGIST

Mikhail Botvinnik vs. Milan Vidmar, Nottingham 1936

Queen's Gambit Declined

In many Queen Pawn Games, the battle is about an isolated d-pawn. One side tries to play with an isolated queen pawn, an isolani, and the other side tries to play against it. In the following game, Mikhail Botvinnik (1911–1995), father of the Soviet School of Chess, shows us how to play with it. He chooses a plan that produces a passed pawn as well as a strong kingside attack. In the end, the plan works.

1. c4
This begins as an English Opening.

1. ...e6
Black will develop his king-bishop through the center.

2. Nf3   d5

3. d4
Now the opening has transposed into a Queen's Gambit.

3. ...Nf6

4. Bg5
Pinning the knight.

4. ...Be7
Breaking the pin.

5. Nc3   0–0
Black has castled quickly.

6. e3
Now the king-bishop can come out.

6. ...Nbd7
Black keeps his c-pawn unblocked. None of this is unusual so far.

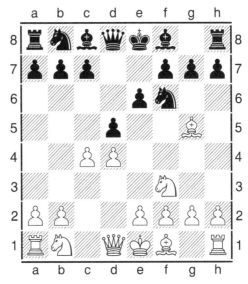

Black to move after 4. Bg5

7. Bd3
Aiming at Black's king-side.

7. ...c5
This pawn advance gives the position a lot of tension. Someone may wind up with an isolated d-pawn.

8. 0–0   cxd4
Vidmar makes the first central capture.

9. exd4   dxc4

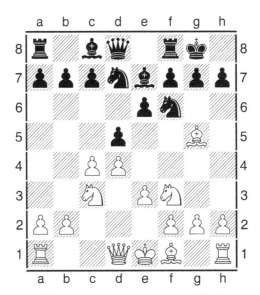

White to move after 6. ...Nbd7

87

10. Bxc4
Sure enough, Botvinnik has accepted an isolated d-pawn.

10. ...Nb6
As a rule of thumb, the defender should try to guard the square in front of the isolated d-pawn, preventing its advance.

11. Bb3
Retreating, but still targeting d5.

11. ...Bd7
The bishop is headed for c6.

Black to move after 10. Bxc4

12. Qd3
Botvinnik introduces his plan.

12. ...Nbd5
Black blockades the d-pawn so it can't move.

13. Ne5
White correctly uses the d-pawn to support a knight across the frontier line.

13. ...Bc6
Vidmar is not afraid of accepting an isolated c-pawn. He feels that this will make it harder for White to advance his d-pawn.

Black to move after 12. Qd3

88

14. Rad1
Most players would naturally place this rook on the open c-file, but Botvinnik's plan requires that the d4-pawn be protected.

14. …Nb4
Attacking the queen.

15. Qh3
The queen shifts across the board to the kingside. From h3, it observes h7, f5, and e6. It's ideally placed here.

15. …Bd5
Occupying the blockade square.

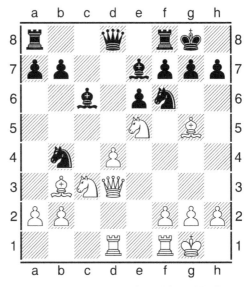

White to move after 14. …Nb4

16. Nxd5   Nbxd5
Black still has a blockade on White's d-pawn.

17. f4
This shows another part of Botvinnik's plan. He's going to advance the f-pawn to f5, attacking e6.

17. …Rc8
Developing the rook to the open c-file.

18. f5
This advance forces a trade.

18. …exf5

19. Rxf5

The result of Botvinnik's plan is that the isolated d-pawn has become a passed pawn.

19. ...Qd6

Botvinnik was a strategist, but he was also a tactician. He quickly finds a refutation of Black's last move.

20. Nxf7!   Rxf7

21. Bxf6   Bxf6

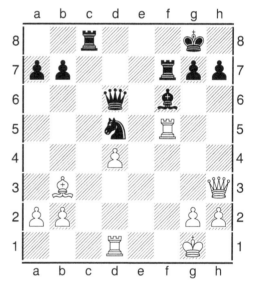

Black to move after 19. Rxf5

22. Rxd5

White has a triple attack: to the queen, to the c8-rook, and indirectly to the f7-rook.

22. ...Qc6

Defending the c8-rook.

23. Rd6

QUESTION 13: Would 23. Rc5 have been better?

23. ...Qe8

Guarding c8 and f7.

White to move after 21. ...Bxf6

24. Rd7

The pig (a rook on the 7th rank) decides matters. Black's position is resignable. So . . .

Black resigns (1–0)

I will always remember how Botvinnik's queen shifted across the 3rd rank.

LESSONS LEARNED

* If you have an isolated pawn, make it a passed pawn.

* If you're playing against an isolated pawn, blockade it.

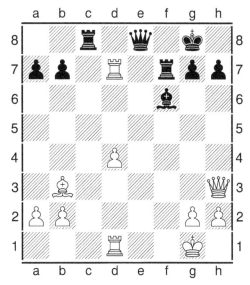

Black to move after 24. Rd7

<u>My Favorite Move</u>   **20. Nxf7!**

GAME 13
CENTRAL CONTROL

Mark Stolberg vs. Mikhail Botvinnik, Moscow 1940

The Nimzo-Indian Defense

The beauty of Mikhail Botvinnik's play is that it's clear. Once he selects a plan, he sets about completing it with exact and precise maneuvering. He doesn't get sidetracked. In his game against Mark Stolberg (1922–1942), the center becomes fixed early on. Botvinnik then plays to occupy his strongpoints. He does so with lethal accuracy.

1. d4   Nf6

2. c4   e6

3. Nc3

3. ...Bb4
The Nimzo-Indian
Defense, named after
Nimzowitsch.

4. e3
The Rubinstein Variation.

4. ...0-0
Botvinnik has castled in
four moves. That's rapid
development!

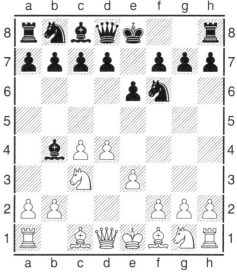

Black to move after 4. e3

5. Bd3
By developing the bishop, White has the option of placing his king-knight on e2 or f3.

5. ...d5
Black continues to fight for control of e4.

6. Nge2
Stolberg decides on e2.

6. ...c5
Getting some activity against the center.

7. 0-0   Nc6
Pressure against the center mounts.

8. cxd5   exd5
The exchanges have cleared a diagonal for the c8-bishop.

9. a3
Putting the question to the bishop.

9. ...cxd4

10. exd4
The center pawns are now fixed, one for each side. The correct plan is to occupy the strongpoints.

10. ...Bd6
Botvinnik keeps his bishop. It guards both of White's strongpoints, c5 and e5.

11. h3
Preventing Black pieces from invading on g4.

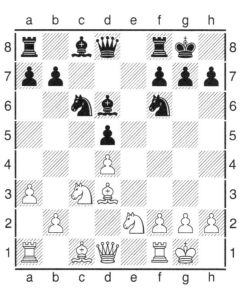

White to move after 10. ...Bd6

11. ...h6
In turn, Botvinnik stops the possible pinning move Bc1-g5.

12. b4
This move reduces the scope of White's dark-square bishop.

12. ...Re8
Botvinnik stays on target. He takes the open file and guards e4, one of his strongpoints.

13. Qb3
Increasing force against d5.

13. ...Be6
Defending d5.

14. Bd2
A quiet development, but it does connect the rooks.

14. ...Qd7
Botvinnik connects his rooks, as well.

15. f4
White attacks, but he creates weakness. He no longer is able to guard e4 with a pawn. The square e4 is a Botvinnikian strongpoint.

15. ...Bf5
Botvinnik stops the advance 16. f5, while fighting for his e4 strongpoint.

16. Qc2
Threatening the f5-bishop.

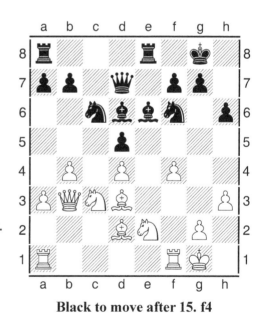

Black to move after 15. f4

16. ...Be4
The future champion occupies his central strongpoint.

17. b5
A positional mistake. Black now has a way to reach his other strongpoint at c4. He can maneuver his knight to a5 and then c4.

17. ...Bxd3!
This is the 3rd move in a row for Black's queen-bishop. But Botvinnik realizes that time is less important in such a position. It's more important to occupy the strongpoints.

18. Qxd3

18. ...Na5
Black is planning to play Nc4 to get a good outpost square for his knight.

19. Ng3
Guarding e4.

19. ...Nc4
Black has acquired the Nc4 outpost, as planned.

20. Bc1
White had to defend his a-pawn. He doesn't want to play a3-a4. That would give up control of b4.

20. ...Rac8
Rooks belong on open files. Black also overprotects his c4 strongpoint.

21. Ra2
White struggles to activate his queen-rook.

21. ...Bf8
Black's queen now defends the d-pawn directly.

22. a4
Giving up control of b4.

22. ...Bb4!
Again, time is not so important. It doesn't matter that Black's dark-square bishop has moved a number of times.

23. Nd1
Botvinnik was threatening to capture on c3, removing a defender of e4.

23. ...Ne4
Botvinnik moves into his strongpoint.

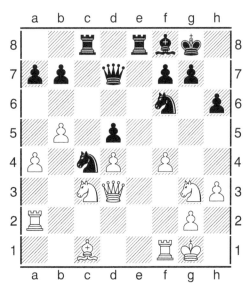

Black to move after 22. a4

24. f5 Nxg3
Black gets rid of another guard on the e4 strongpoint.

25. Qxg3 Bd6
As before, Botvinnik shows that time is not as critical as it is in fully open positions. He can move the same piece several times to complete his plans.

26. Qf3 Be7
Planning to reposition the bishop to f6.

27. Qg3
Threatening to capture on h6 because of the g-file pin.

27. ...Bf6
Botvinnik is not afraid of the threat to h6.

28. Bxh6
Trading a wing pawn for a center pawn. Center pawns are better.

28. ...Bxd4+
Now Black has full control over the center, and White can't do anything about it.

29. Kh1   f6
Black's queen now guards g7.

QUESTION 14: Why didn't Black play 29… Re4?

30. Bc1
Undeveloping to the home rank.

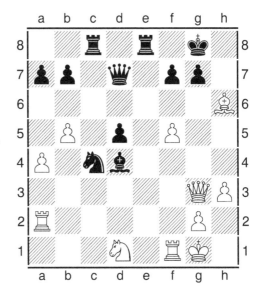

White to move after 28. ...Bxd4+

30. ...Re4!
Occupying the e4 strongpoint.

31. Qd3   Ne5
Who controls the center? Botvinnik!

32. Qb1
More retreating.

32. ...Rc4!
Black has all his pieces in the center, and they are very active. White's pieces are like a fish out of water: they are poorly placed.

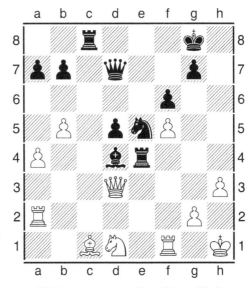

White to move after 31. ...Ne5

33. a5　　Bc5
A nice central pattern.
Black owns the center.

34. b6
White's big counterattack.

34. ...a6
White's "big" counterat-
tack is easily refuted.

35. Nb2
The knight crawls off the
home rank.

35. ...Rc3
Invading further.

36. Bd2
More crawling.

36. ...Rb3
Pinning the knight.

37. Qc2　　Qb5
Finally, the Black queen
becomes menacing, as
well.

38. Rc1
White can still find
threats.

38. ...Bf8
How many times has this
bishop moved? It doesn't
matter!

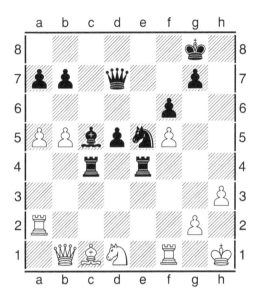

White to move after 33. ...Bc5

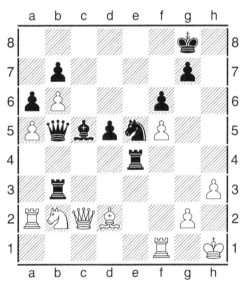

White to move after 37. ...Qb5

39. Rd1

39. ...Re2
It's time to get a pig. Black
secures the 7th rank.

40. Qc1

40. ...Rxh3+!
A deadly and explosive
move!

41. gxh3
White's 2nd rank has been
ripped open.

41. ...d4!
Black is planning Qd5,
and there's no stopping it.
White is doomed!

White resigns (0-1)

I will always remember
how Botvinnik put his
pieces in the center of the
board.

LESSONS LEARNED

* In fixed centers, occupy
your strongpoints.

* Sometimes, time is less
important than squares.

* Don't change your plans
without good reason.

<u>My Favorite Move</u>

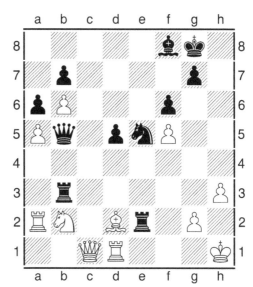

Black to move after 40. Qc1

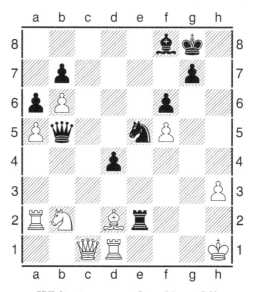

White to move after 41. ...d4!

32. ...Rc4!

GAME 14
CASTLING INTO DANGER

Paul Keres vs. Mikhail Botvinnik, Leningrad 1941

The Nimzo-Indian Defense

Paul Keres (1916-1975) was a fantastic player. He won the 1938 AVRO Tournament ahead of Reuben Fine (1914-1993) on tiebreaks. At that time, it was the strongest tournament ever. But there was one player with whom Keres had trouble: the great Botvinnik. Watch what Botvinnik does to him in this game.

1. d4   Nf6

2. c4   e6

3. Nc3   Bb4
The Nimzo-Indian Defense.

4. Qc2
Keres plays to avoid doubled pawns.

4. ...d5
In a surprising way, this move attacks d4 indirectly by possible discovery.

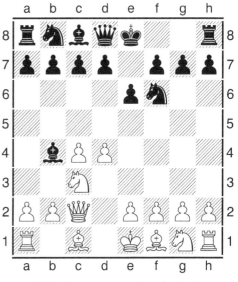

Black to move after 4. Qc2

5. cxd5   exd5

The center is now fixed.

6. Bg5   h6

Putting the question to the bishop: will it take the f6-knight or retreat?

7. Bh4   c5

The play is starting to get sharp.

8. 0–0–0

Is the queenside safe?

8. ...Bxc3

Botvinnik takes control.

9. Qxc3   g5

Breaking the pin.

10. Bg3   cxd4

Botvinnik quickly has command.

11. Qxd4   Nc6

Developing with a gain of time.

12. Qa4

Pinning the knight.

12. ...Bf5

Black's bishop cuts across the board.

13. e3   Rc8

The White king is in an unpleasant position. White has castled into a big attack.

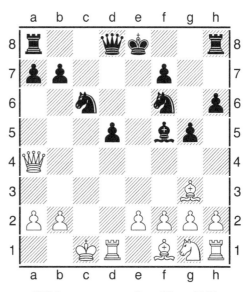

White to move after 12. ...Bf5

14. Bd3
The White king hopes to find shelter at b1.

14. ...Qd7
Defending the bishop and breaking the pin.

15. Kb1   Bxd3+

16. Rxd3   Qf5
A powerful pin. The queen has replaced the bishop.

17. e4
A pawn sacrifice to gain defensive time.

17. ...Nxe4
Taking with a piece to keep the lines open.

18. Ka1

White to move after 16. ...Qf5

Black's king is still in the center, but White's king is in more immediate danger.

18. ...0–0
Black finally castles on move 18.

19. Rd1
White retreats the rook. He was afraid of a potential discovery on it.

19. ...b5!
Botvinnik can afford this
pawn sacrifice.

20. Qxb5   Nd4

21. Qd3

<u>QUESTION 15</u>: Why
didn't White take the
knight, 21. Rxd4?

21. ...Nc2+

22. Kb1
There is something ele-
gant about the diagonal
b1-f5.

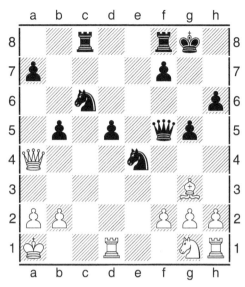

White to move after 19. ...b5!

22. ...Nb4
This last move is crushing. White's queen must move off the long
diagonal. After that, there's no answer to Nd2+.

White resigns (0-1)

I will always remember
Botvinnik's consistent
initiative.

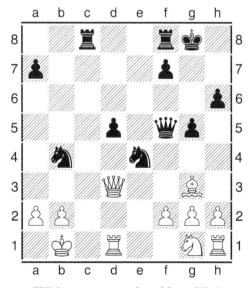

White to move after 22. ...Nb4

LESSONS LEARNED

* You don't have to castle early if it is unnecessary.

* Be careful which side you castle on.

* Some trades can actually help the attack.

My Favorite Move   19. …b5!

GAME 15
GAME OF THE CENTURY

Donald Byrne vs. Robert Fischer, New York 1956

The Gruenfeld Defense

The story was news around the world. A 13-year-old boy played a truly extraordinary game, involving an ingenious queen sacrifice. It was soon dubbed the Game of the Century. That same boy, Robert (Bobby) Fischer (1943–2008), would go on to be the youngest Grandmaster in history (up to that point), the winner of eight U.S. Championships (all eight times he played), and the 11th official world chess champion.

1. Nf3
It starts as a Reti Opening.

1. …Nf6

2. c4   g6
Fischer flanks.

3. Nc3   Bg7

4. d4
Now it's transposed into a queen-pawn game.

4. …0-0
Fischer has castled quickly.

5. Bf4   d5

By transposition, we finally have a Gruenfeld Defense.

6. Qb3

A popular variation at the time.

6. ...dxc4

Fischer takes, making the white queen move again.

7. Qxc4

Byrne is happy, having two pawns in the center vs. one.

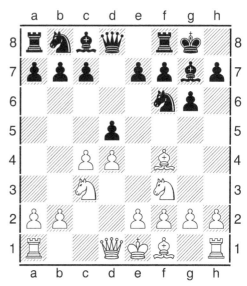

White to move after 5. ...d5

7. ...c6

Moving the c-pawn to safety.

8. e4

White gets a classical pawn center.

8. ...Nbd7

9. Rd1

White supports his d-pawn.

9. ...Nb6

Making the queen move again.

10. Qc5   Bg4

Fischer has a clever idea in mind.

11. Bg5?   Na4!!

A great move. If Nxa4, then Nxe4. White's position would not be so good.

12. Qa3

White is smart. He does not take the knight.

12. ...Nxc3

13. bxc3   Nxe4

Fischer's capture on e4 looks questionable. It seems to allow a fork on e7.

White to move after 10. ...Bg4

14. Bxe7

How is Fischer going to answer this double attack?

14. ...Qb6!

Having lost his e-pawn, Fischer will get tremendous play on the e-file.

White to move after 14. ...Qb6!

15. Bc4   Nxc3!
Now on 16, Qxc3, Black
has 16…Rfe8.

16. Bc5
Attacking the queen.

16. …Rfe8+
Saving the rook with a
check.

17. Kf1
White loses the right to
castle.

17. …Be6!!
A queen sacrifice for a
deep purpose. It is this
move – 17…Be6!! – that
makes this game so famous.

18. Bxb6
White takes the queen
anyway.

18. …Bxc4+
The bishop falls with
check.

19. Kg1   Ne2+

20. Kf1   Nxd4+
The discovery lets Black
take an important pawn
for free.

21. Kg1   Ne2+
Setting up another dis-
covery.

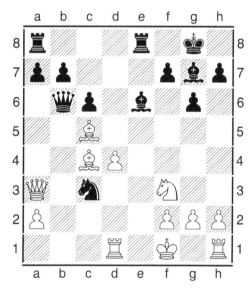

White to move after 15. …Nxc3!

White to move after 17. …Be6!!

22. Kf1   Nc3+

On c3, the knight is defended by the g7-bishop. That's why Black had to win the d4-pawn.

23. Kg1   axb6

Threatening White's queen.

24. Qb4   Ra4!

Defending the c4-bishop with a gain of time. Now we see why it was crucial to put the knight on c3.

25. Qxb6   Nxd1

Thank you for the rook.

26. h3

Making *luft* for the king.

26. ...Rxa2

Pigging out.

27. Kh2   Nxf2

The knight gets back into action.

28. Re1   Rxe1

29. Qd8+

Before taking back, White plays a *zwischenzug*.

29. ...Bf8

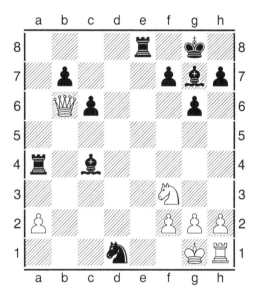

White to move after 25. ...Nxd1

30. Nxe1   Bd5
Fischer makes sure his
bishop is safe.

31. Nf3   Ne4
The knight is centralized
and defended.

32. Qb8   b5
Now all of Black's pieces
and pawns are secure.

33. h4   h5
Stopping further h-file
advances.

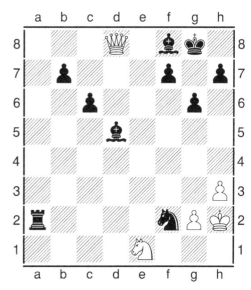

White to move after 30. …Bd5

34. Ne5   Kg7
Now the f8-bishop is free
to move.

35. Kg1

QUESTION 16: Why did
White play 35. Kg1?

35. …Bc5+
The king hunt begins.

36. Kf1   Ng3+

37. Ke1   Bb4+

38. Kd1   Bb3+
Mate is forced.

39. Kc1   Ne2+

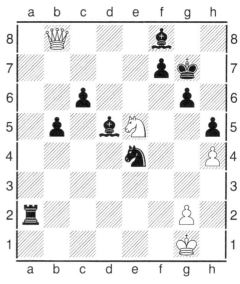

Black to move after 35. Kg1

40. Kb1   Nc3+

41. Kc1   Rc2 mate!
It was a fantastically well-played game by Fischer. Fischer's other mate was 41...Ba3#.

Black wins (0-1)

I will always remember how Fischer's queenless forces became an overwhelming army.

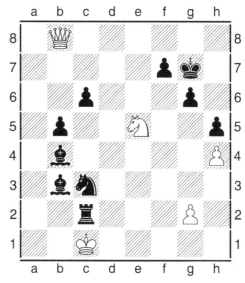

White is mated after 41. ...Rc2

LESSONS LEARNED

* Don't sacrifice without justification.

* Don't take any opponent for granted.

* A team of pieces can be better than a queen.

My Favorite Move   17. ...Be6!!

GAME 16
THE WRONG ROOK

Robert Byrne vs. Robert Fischer, New York 1963-64

The King's Indian Defense, Fianchetto Variation

It's a famous story. In the analysis room, after Fischer played his 21st move, the grandmasters were saying he should resign. Supposedly, they said his position was lost. Then the news came in. Fischer didn't resign. His opponent did! Obviously, we can't always trust expert opinion.

1. d4   Nf6

2. c4   g6
Fischer decides to flank his king-bishop.

3. g3
Byrne decides to flank his king-bishop, as well.

3. …c6

4. Bg2   d5
This idea is also seen in the Gruenfeld Defense.

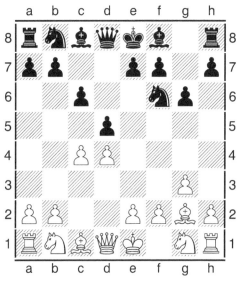

White to move after 4. …d5

5. cxd5   cxd5

The players have exchanged c-pawns for d-pawns.

6. Nc3   Bg7

7. e3   0–0

8. Nge2   Nc6

The main difference is the placement of the king-knights. Black's pieces are more active.

9. 0–0   b6

Time to develop the queen-bishop.

10. b3

White also thinks it's time to develop the queen-bishop.

White to move after 8. ...Nc6

10. ...Ba6

Somehow, Black has gained a move on White.

The lost move was White's 7. e3. Black hasn't moved his king-pawn yet.

11. Ba3

It may look fairly symmetrical, but Black has more active chances.

11. ...Re8

12. Qd2

12. ...e5!
Now the king-pawn
moves!

13. dxe5   Nxe5
White has given Black
an isolated d-pawn, but
Black has more active
pieces.

14. Rfd1?
White immediately hits at
Black's isolated d-pawn.
But he does it with the
wrong rook!

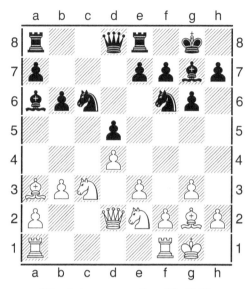

Black to move after 12. Qd2

<u>QUESTION 17</u>: Why might 14. Rad1 be safer than Rfd1?

14. ...Nd3!
A nasty knight invasion.

15. Qc2
But now the knight is
threatened.

15. ...Nxf2!
Now we see the problem
with 14. Rfd1. It weak-
ened f2. White should
have played 14. Rad1
instead.

16. Kxf2   Ng4+

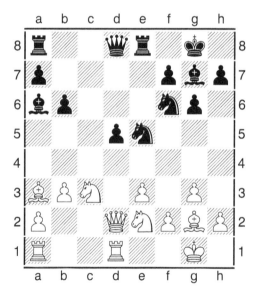

Black to move after 14. Rfd1?

17. Kg1   Nxe3

Fischer will get a rook and two pawns for the two knights. On paper, it's almost even.

18. Qd2

18. …Nxg2!
Another Fischer surprise! Instead of taking the Exchange, he gets rid of a key defender of White's kingside.

19. Kxg2   d4!
Fischer wants to open lines for attack. So he sacrifices a pawn.

20. Nxd4   Bb7+

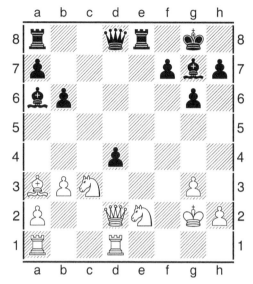

White to move after 19. …d4!

21. Kf1   Qd7!
It was at this point that the grandmasters decided Fischer was losing and should resign. Instead, Byrne resigned!

Byrne was in fact losing. If 22. Qf2, then 22… Qh3+ 23. Kg1 Re1+!! 24. Rxe1 Bxd4 wins. If instead 22. Ndb5, then 22… Qh3+ 23. Kg1 Bh6 wins.

White resigns (0–1)

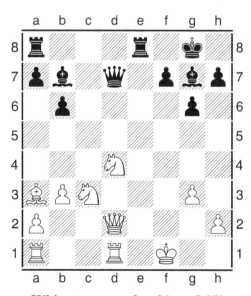

White to move after 21. …Qd7!

I will always remember Byrne's fatal rook move.

LESSONS LEARNED

* Small differences in symmetrical positions are important.

*Try to use the right rook.

My Favorite Move   18. …Nxg2!

GAME 17
AN AMAZING ROOK MOVE

Bent Larsen vs. Boris Spassky, Belgrade 1970

The Nimzo-Larsen Attack

The ten top players from the Soviet Union are playing the ten top players from the rest of the world. Board one has Bent Larsen (1935–2010) of Denmark. He's facing World Champion Boris Spassky (b. 1937). What follows is one of the greatest moments of brilliance in chess history. It's also my favorite game.

1. b3
This is the Nimzo-Larsen Attack. It's named after Nimzowitsch and Larsen.

1. ...e5
A straightforward pawn move, right to the center.

2. Bb2
A hypermodern idea. White tries to control the center before occupying it. Here, he flanks his bishop. This is called a *fianchetto*.

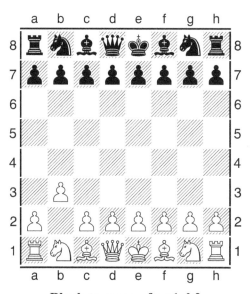

Black to move after 1. b3

2. ...Nc6
Developing toward the center.

3. c4
Now White attacks d5. Is he playing a dark-square game or a light-square game?

3. ...Nf6
Black goes for more direct development.

4. Nf3
Hoping that Black overextends himself by advancing the e-pawn.

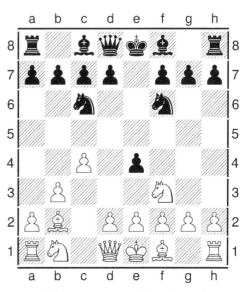

White to move after 4. ...e4

4. ...e4
Spassky obliges him.

5. Nd4   Bc5
Spassky continues to develop.

6. Nxc6   dxc6
Taking away from the center to open the d-file.

7. e3   Bf5
More development, protecting the e-pawn.

8. Qc2   Qe7
Overprotecting the e-pawn and preparing queenside castling.

9. Be2   0–0–0

10. f4?

<u>QUESTION 18:</u> What happens if Black captures the pawn *en passant*, 10... exf3?

10. ...Ng4
The attack begins.

11. g3
Stopping a queen invasion at h4. White doesn't have time for this.

11. ...h5!
Every Black piece is in action. The g3-pawn is now a target.

12. h3   h4!
Spassky ignores the threat. He keeps attacking. This h-pawn is dangerous.

White to move after 7. ...Bf5

White to move after 12. ...h4!

13. hxg4   hxg3

14. Rg1   Rh1!!
An unbelievable move! Nothing protects the black rook.

15. Rxh1   g2
A mighty threat.

16. Rf1
16. Rg1 Qh4+ is no better, when 17. Kd1 is met by 17...Qh1.

16...Qh4+

17. Kd1   gxf1Q+
It's mate in three moves.

White resigns (0-1)

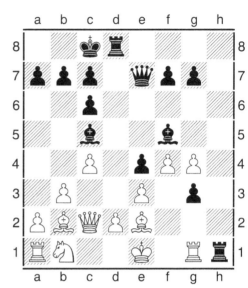

White to move after 14. ...Rh1!!

I will always remember the unexpectedly brilliant Rh1 move.

LESSONS LEARNED

* Value attack over material.

* An advancing pawn can be a serious threat.

My Favorite Move

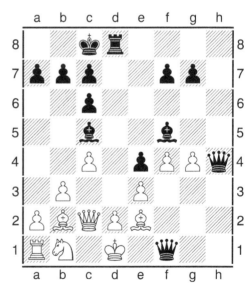

White to move after 17. ...gxf1Q+

14. ...Rh1!!

GAME 18
SUDDEN COLLAPSE

Boris Spassky vs. Robert Fischer, Reykjavik 1972

The Nimzo-Indian Defense

The World Championship of 1972 was the greatest spectacle in the history of chess. Could an American defeat the Soviet system? The Russians had dominated top level chess for 24 years. With this crushing victory in Game 5, Bobby Fischer tied his match with Boris Spassky. He also showed he had the right stuff to take the title.

1. d4   Nf6

2. c4   e6

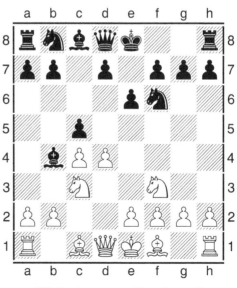

White to move after 4. ...c5

3. Nc3   Bb4
Pinning the knight. This is the Nimzo-Indian Defense. Black fights for e4 with pieces.

4. Nf3   c5
A typical move in d-pawn games.

5. e3
Supporting his d-pawn and letting out the king-bishop.

5. ...Nc6
Pressuring the center.

6. Bd3
Aiming at the kingside and guarding e4.

6. ...Bxc3+
Black trades bishop for knight to create doubled c-pawns.

7. bxc3   d6
Fischer's plan is to advance the e-pawn.

8. e4
Advancing his own e-pawn and clearing the way for the queen-bishop.

8. ...e5
Fischer is willing to allow the center to become closed.

9. d5
Black didn't exchange on d4. He didn't want to allow White to get rid of a doubled c-pawn.

9. ...Ne7
Shifting over to the king-side. The square g6 looks inviting.

White to move after 8. ...e5

10. Nh4
Spassky unblocks the f-pawn so he can advance it.

10. ...h6
Preventing Bg5 and also making g7-g5 possible.

11. f4

Spassky plays to open the f-file.

QUESTION 19: Does Black win a piece by 11...exf4 12. Bxf4 g5?

11. ...Ng6

Fischer is not afraid to accept his own doubled pawns.

12. Nxg6   fxg6

Black has doubled g-pawns, but these will become useful.

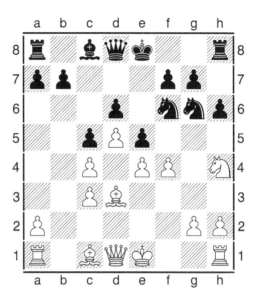

White to move after 11. ...Ng6

13. fxe5

White creates a protected passed pawn at d5. But White's d-pawn will go nowhere.

13. ...dxe5

Although Black has doubled g-pawns and an isolated e-pawn, he has the better pawn structure. It's more harmonious for his bishop.

14. Be3

Attacking the c-pawn.

14. ...b6

Protecting the c-pawn.

White to move after 13. ...dxe5

123

15. 0-0   0-0
Finally, both players have castled.

16. a4
Hoping to play a5.

16. ...a5!
Accepting a backward b-pawn, but fixing the a4 target. This is ultimately important.

17. Rb1
Rooks belong on open and half-open files.

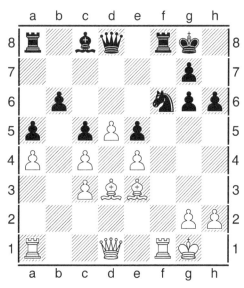

White to move after 16. ...a5!

17. ...Bd7
Fischer keeps his eyes on the prize.

18. Rb2
White may double rooks on the b-file or the f-file.

18. ...Rb8
Now Black's queen is free to move.

19. Rbf2
Doubling on the f-file.

19. ...Qe7
Clearing the home rank, so the rooks defend each other.

20. Bc2
At c2, the bishop guards a4 and e4.

Black to move after 20. Bc2

20. ...g5

Note that all black pawns are on dark squares. They don't get in the way of the light-square bishop. That really is harmony. White has the two bishops, but they have limited scope.

21. Bd2

The bishop is safer at d2. But it has poor mobility.

21. ...Qe8

Fischer piles up on the a4-target. He also has another idea in mind.

22. Be1

It almost seems as if White is just making moves, with no plan.

22. ...Qg6!

Now e4 is under pressure, as well as a4.

23. Qd3

Protecting e4.

23. ...Nh5

Allowing rooks to be traded.

24. Rxf8+   Rxf8

25. Rxf8+   Kxf8

Black's king is not badly placed here. It can always hide at e7.

26. Bd1   Nf4

Attacking the queen. Where will it go?

27. Qc2?

Under pressure, Spassky blunders.

27. ...Bxa4!

Played instantly. It's said that Spassky slumped in his chair after Fischer played his move.

If 28. Qxa4, then 28... Qxe4 is crushing. For example, if 29. Kf2, there would follow 29...Nd3+ 30. Kg3 Qh4+ 31. Kf3 Qf4+ 32. Ke2 Nc1 mate!

White resigns (0–1)

I will always remember how Fischer took advantage of Spassky's pawn weaknesses.

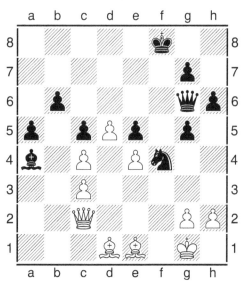

White to move after 27. ...Bxa4!

LESSONS LEARNED

* Fix the targets you intend to attack.

* Don't put your pawns on the same color as your bishop.

* Knights can be better than bishops in blocked positions.

<u>My Favorite Move</u>   27. ...Bxa4!

GAME 19
THE DRAGON IS SLAIN

Anatoly Karpov vs. Viktor Korchnoi, Moscow 1974

The Sicilian Defense, Dragon Variation

The final Candidates Match of 1974 was fought between Anatoly Karpov (b. 1951) and Viktor Korchnoi (1931–2016). The winner would face Bobby Fischer for the world title. Karpov eventually won the match by one game, including the following magnificent victory in the second round. Karpov didn't know that he would soon be declared World Champion. But Karpov didn't have to play Fischer in even a single game, since Bobby forfeited his crown.

1. e4   c5
The Sicilian Defense.

2. Nf3   d6
To fight for e5.

3. d4   cxd4

4. Nxd4   Nf6

5. Nc3   g6
The Dragon Variation. Supposedly, Black's pieces and pawns trace the outline of a dragon's winding tail. In chess, you need a vivid imagination.

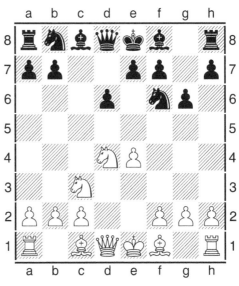

White to move after 5. …g6

6. Be3   Bg7

QUESTION 20: What happens after 6...Ng4?

7. f3
Protecting e4 and stopping Nf6-g4.

7. ...Nc6

8. Qd2
Doubling on the c1-h6 diagonal.

8. ...0–0

9. Bc4
On c4, White's bishop discourages Black from playing his main freeing move, d6-d5.

9. ...Bd7

10. h4
White plans to open the h-file for attack.

10. ...Rc8
Black tries to use the half-open c-file in the Sicilian.

11. Bb3

QUESTION 21: How does play continue after 11. 0-0-0?

11. ...Ne5
In the Sicilian Defense, the square c4 is often useful for Black.

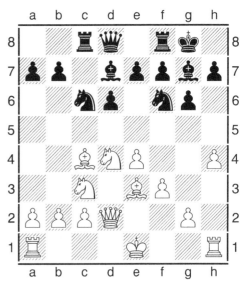

White to move after 10. ...Rc8

12. 0–0–0
When castled on opposite sides, both players can attack the enemy king more freely.

12. …Nc4
The knight comes into the strong c4 target square.

13. Bxc4   Rxc4

14. h5
If instead White plays 14. Bh6, he loses material to 14…Rxd4.

14. …Nxh5

15. g4
The h-file is now open.

15. …Nf6

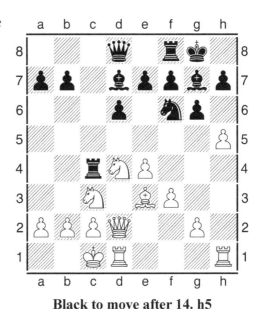

Black to move after 14. h5

16. Nde2
This retreat safeguards White's position.

16. …Qa5

17. Bh6   Bxh6

18. Qxh6   Rfc8
Doubling rooks on the c-file.

19. Rd3
White defends his position a bit more before continuing.

19. ...R4c5
Trying to stop White
from playing g4-g5.

20. g5!
Karpov plays it anyway!

20. ...Rxg5

21. Rd5!
Black must trade rooks.

21. ...Rxd5

22. Nxd5
If Black's knight takes
White's, Black gets mated.

22. ...Re8
Defending e7.

23. Nef4   Bc6

24. e5!
Karpov obstructs the 5th
rank.

24. ...Bxd5

25. exf6
Threatening mate at g7.

25. ...exf6

26. Qxh7+   Kf8

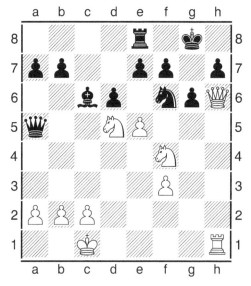

White to move after 19. ...R4c5

Black to move after 24. e5!

27. Qh8+

After 27…Ke7 28. Nxd5+ Qxd5 29. Re1+, Black's position is hopeless.

Black resigns (1–0)

I will always remember Karpov's 5th rank obstruction.

LESSONS LEARNED

* Safeguard your position before continuing the attack.

* When castled on opposite sides, go after the enemy king.

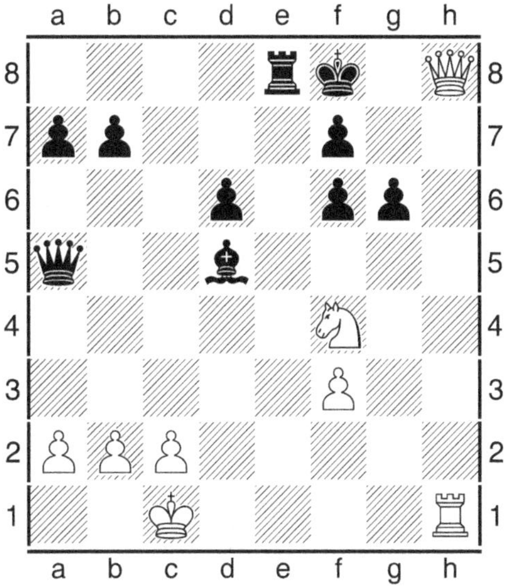

<u>My Favorite Move</u>

Black to move after 27. Qh8+

21. Rd5!

GAME 20
THE DOUBLE BISHOP SACRIFICE

Garry Kasparov vs. Lajos Portisch, Niksic 1983

The Queen's Indian Defense

Chess has its incredible attackers. They often rely on sacrifices. Not all sacrifices are correct. Some attackers succeed because of poor defense. Garry Kasparov (b. 1963) is different. His sacrifices are almost always correct. His opponents often seem helpless. In this game, Kasparov puts away Lajos Portisch (b. 1937) with inspired brilliance.

1. d4   Nf6

2. c4   e6

3. Nf3
White delays playing 3. Nc3 to avoid 3…Bb4.

3. …b6
The Queen's Indian Defense.

4. Nc3   Bb7
Black fights for control of e4. He also could have continued with 4...Bb4.

5. a3
To prevent the pin at b4.

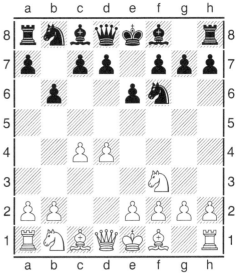

White to move after 3. …b6

5. ...d5
Still fighting for e4.

6. cxd5   Nxd5
Seeking a trade of knights.

7. e3
Letting out the king-bishop.

7. ...Nxc3

8. bxc3   Be7
Black is getting ready to castle.

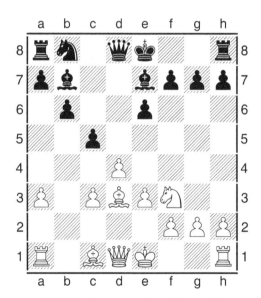

White to move after 8. ...Be7

9. Bb5+
A check. White wants to see how Black responds.

9. ...c6

10. Bd3   c5
This position could have been reached without the 9th move for either side.

11. 0–0   Nc6

12. Bb2
Right now, the bishop doesn't seem effective at b2. But wait until later! The move reminds me of

White to move after 10. ...c5

the way Botvinnik developed his queen-bishop against Capablanca in the 1938 AVRO tournament.

12. ...Rc8
Black expects the c-file to open.

13. Qe2
Connecting the rooks.
Now they defend each
other.

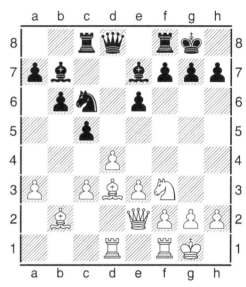

Black to move after 14. Rad1

13. ...0-0
White's bishops are aimed
at Black's kingside. If the
lines are opened, they
could become dangerous.

14. Rad1
A good developing move,
with a hidden threat.

QUESTION 22: What
does 14. Rad1 threaten?

14. ...Qc7
Getting the queen off the d-file.

15. c4!
Suddenly, the b2-bishop
has joined the fight.

15. ...cxd4

16. exd4
Opening the e-file.

16. ...Na5
Black's pieces are set up
for a queenside attack. His
kingside seems inviting.

17. d5!
Kasparov advances a
pawn to open the lines.

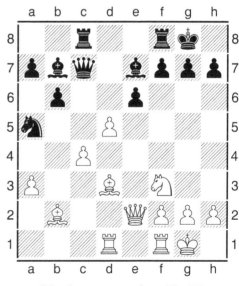

Black to move after 17. d5!

17. ...exd5

18. cxd5   Bxd5
The position is about to explode.

19. Bxh7+!
The attack begins!

19. ...Kxh7

20. Rxd5   Kg8
Portisch tries to find shelter for his king.

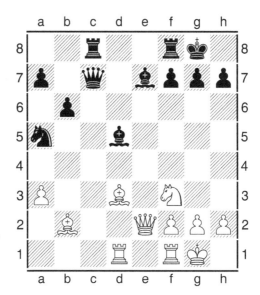

White to move after 18. ...Bxd5

21. Bxg7!!
There is no shelter when facing a wizard like Kasparov.

21. ...Kxg7
Black's king has lost his clothes. He has no pawn cover.

22. Ne5!
Invading and unblocking the queen's diagonal.

22. ...Rfd8
Making the f8-square available for escape.

23. Qg4+   Kf8

24. Qf5
Threatening mate at f7.

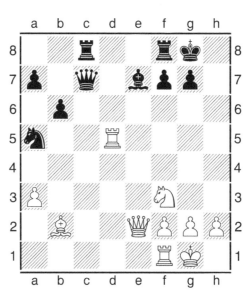

White to move after 20. ...Kg8

24. ...f6

25. Nd7+
White has various mating threats.

25. ...Rxd7
Black hopes to survive by giving up the Exchange.

26. Rxd7
Capturing with pig power.

26. ...Qc5
Keeping e7 guarded.

27. Qh7
White gets a super pig: the queen!

27. ...Rc7

28. Qh8+!
Kasparov avoids the trick. If 28. Rd3?, then 28... Qxf2+!! 29. Kxf2 (29. Rxf2 Rc1+) 29...Bc5+ 30. Kg3 Rxh7, and Black has held.

28. ...Kf7

29. Rd3!
Advancing backwards! From d3, the rook is set up to move along the 3rd rank.

29. ...Nc4

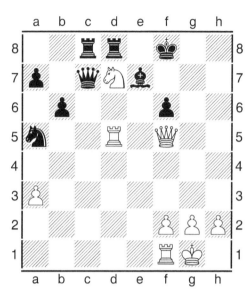

Black to move after 25. Nd7+

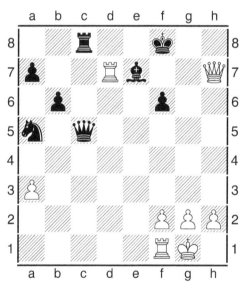

Black to move after 27. Qh7

30. Rfd1!
Doubling rooks.

30. ...Ne5?
On 30...Bd6, Kasparov had 31. Rd5 Qxa3 32. Rxd6 Nxd6 33. Qh7+, skewering king and rook.

31. Qh7+   Ke6

32. Qg8+   Kf5

33. g4+
A wonderful king hunt.

33. ...Kf4

34. Rd4+   Kf3

35. Qb3+
If 35...Qc3, White wins Black's queen by a rook check on d3. Or if 35... Ke2, then 36. Qe3 is mate.

Black resigns (1–0)

I will always remember how Kasparov destroyed Black's kingside pawns.

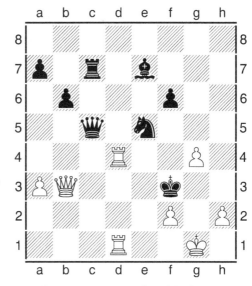

Black to move after 35. Qb3+

LESSONS LEARNED

* Try to destroy the enemy king's pawn cover.

* When winning, watch out for sneaky counterplay.

<u>**My Favorite Move**</u>   **21. Bxg7!!**

GAME 21
THE DEADLY KING

Nigel Short vs. Jan Timman, Tilburg 1991

Alekhine's Defense

This game is about trading. Black, Jan Timman (b. 1951), tries to trade down. With White, Nigel Short (b. 1965), avoids most of those trades. He especially keeps his queen. White's queen then attacks Black's kingside. But even the queen needs help. In the end, that help comes from a surprising piece.

1. e4   Nf6
Alekhine's Defense. It's named after the 4th official world chess champion, Alekhine.

2. e5   Nd5
Going to e4 would be a mistake.

3. d4   d6

4. Nf3
The Four Pawns Attack (4. c4 Nb6 5. f4) used to be popular.

4. …g6
Black decides to flank his king-bishop. Another idea was 4…Bg4.

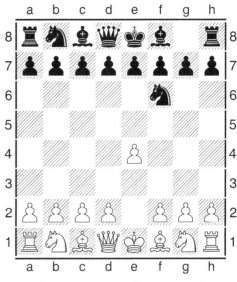

White to move after 1. …Nf6

5. Bc4   Nb6
Attacking the bishop.

6. Bb3   Bg7

7. Qe2
White avoids a trade of
queens.

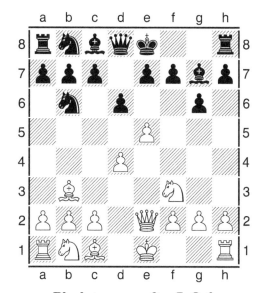

Black to move after 7. Qe2

7. …Nc6

8. 0–0   0–0

9. h3!
Preventing an annoying
pin.

9. …a5
Threatening to trap the
b3-bishop.

10. a4
Stopping the a-pawn's
advance.

10. …dxe5

11. dxe5   Nd4
Black forces a trade of knights.

12. Nxd4   Qxd4

13. Re1
Protecting the e-pawn.

13. …e6

14. Nd2!
The knight is not stopping at d2.

14. ...Nd5

15. Nf3   Qc5

16. Qe4
From e4, the White queen can shift to h4.

16. ...Qb4
Black wants to trade queens. White has attacking chances. He wants to keep his queen on the board.

17. Bc4
Avoiding a queen trade.

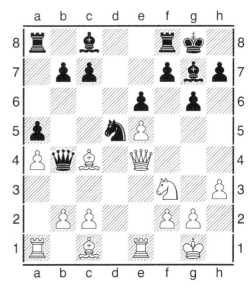

Black to move after 17. Bc4

17. ...Nb6

18. b3
This defends the bishop, but it leads to doubled c-pawns.

18. ...Nxc4

19. bxc4
Naturally, White doesn't play 19. Qxc4.

QUESTION 23: What happens if Black now plays 19...Bd7?

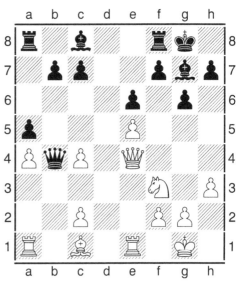

Black to move after 19. bxc4

19. …Re8
Avoiding loss of the Exchange.

20. Rd1   Qc5

21. Qh4
The queen zeroes in on the kingside dark squares.

21. …b6
To flank the queen-bishop.

22. Be3
Gaining time on the Black queen.

22. …Qc6
At c6, the queen is stuck on the queenside. That makes the kingside harder to defend.

23. Bh6
Trying to trade off a key defender of the dark squares.

23. …Bh8
Black avoids the trade.

24. Rd8!
A menacing invasion.

24. …Bb7

25. Rad1
Doubling rooks on the d-file.

25. …Bg7
Black decides he must trade this bishop after all.

26. R8d7!
Now if 26. Bxh6 27. Qxh6 Qe4?, then 27. Rxf7!!, with a mating attack.

26. ...Rf8

27. Bxg7   Kxg7
Black's kingside dark squares have become quite weak.

28. R1d4
A rook lift.

28. ...Rae8

29. Qf6+
The dark squares are defenseless.

29. ...Kg8

30. h4
White hopes to play h4-h5.

30. ...h5
Black's dark squares
are looking weaker and
weaker.

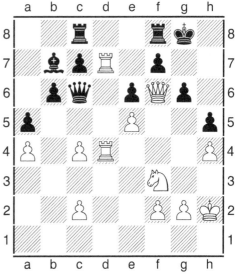

31. Kh2   Rc8
It seems White's attack
needs help. Short finds an
amazing helper.

32. Kg3!   Rce8

33. Kf4!   Bc8

White to move after 31. ...Rc8

142

34. Kg5!!
A forced march!

If 34…Bxd7, White has 35. Kh6! Mate on g7 is then unstoppable.

Black resigns (1–0)

I will always remember Short's long king march up.

LESSONS LEARNED

* The king is a strong piece (as Steinitz maintained).

* Don't weaken the squares around your king.

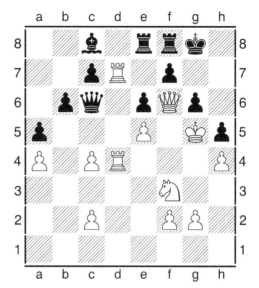

Black to move after 34. Kg5!!

My Favorite Move   34. Kg5!!

GAME 22
FASTER THAN A SPEEDING PAWN

Viswanathan Anand vs. Vassily Ivanchuk, Linares 1993

The Petrov Defense

Born in 1969, former World Champion Viswanathan (Vishy) Anand is known for his chess fighting skills and for his very quick play. In his youth, he always seemed to move twice as fast as his opponents, which made him an outstanding blitz player. His win over the dangerous Vassily Ivanchuk (b. 1969) at Linares in 1993 shows how Anand can develop a sudden winning attack, just like that.

1. e4	**e5**

2. Nf3	**Nf6**

The Petrov Defense.

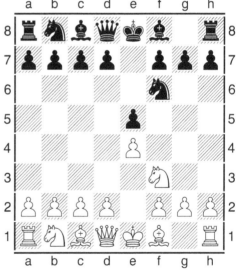

White to move after 2. …Nf6

There is a famous trap here: 3. Nxe5 Nxe4 4. Qe2 Nf6 5. Nc6+, winning the Black queen.

3. d4	**Nxe4**

Black will have to give the pawn back.

4. Bd3	**d5**

5. Nxe5
Material is even again.

5. ...Nd7
Trying to get rid of
White's aggressive knight.

6. Nxd7   Bxd7

7. 0–0   Qh4
Making queenside cas-
tling possible.

8. c4
Trying to undermine the
e4-knight's support and
opening lines.

8. ...0–0–0

9. c5
Preventing Bf8-d6.

9. ...g5
Attacking on the kingside
and making g7 available
to the dark-square bishop.

10. Nc3   Bg7
An unusual *fianchetto*.

11. g3
Trying to weaken Black's
hold on e4.

11. ...Qh3
Entering on the weakened
h3.

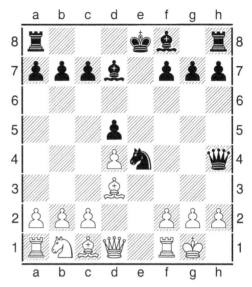

White to move after 7. ...Qh4

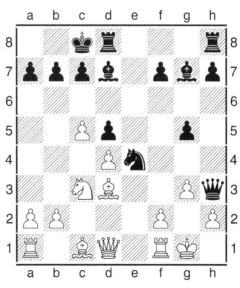

White to move after 11. ...Qh3

145

12. Nxe4   dxe4

13. Bxe4   Bb5
Attacking the rook at f1.

14. Bg2!
Anand kicks out the queen and winds up flanking his bishop.

14. ...Qf5

15. Be3!
Surrendering the Exchange for attack!

15. ...Bxf1

16. Bxf1   Rhe8
Black has good centralization and development.

17. Qa4
Launching the queenside assault. Anand figures his two bishops make up for losing the Exchange.

17. ...Kb8
Protecting a7.

18. Rd1   c6
Overprotecting d5 and preventing c5-c6.

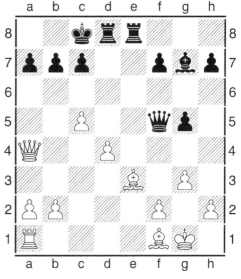

Black to move after 17. Qa4

19. Rd3
A serious rook lift!

19. ...Qe4

20. Ra3   a6
Black had to defend a7. Anand has forced a weakness on Black.

21. Bd3
Gaining a tempo on the queen.

21. ...Qg4

22. Rb3
White's rook is now beautifully poised on the b-file.

22. ...Bxd4
Pawn grabbing.

23. Rxb7+!!
An explosive capture, ripping open the Black's king position.

23. ...Kxb7

24. Qxa6+   Kb8

<u>QUESTION 24</u>: What happens after 24...Kc7?

25. Qb6+   Ka8

26. Qxc6+
Capturing a pawn with check.

26. ...Kb8

27. Qb6+   Ka8

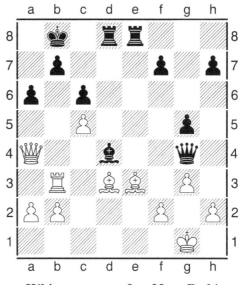

White to move after 22. ...Bxd4

28. Bb5!

Black is going to lose the house.

Black resigns (1–0)

I will always remember how Anand sacrificed his rook.

LESSONS LEARNED

* Two bishops can often make up for losing the Exchange.

* When castled on opposite sides, attack first.

* Pressure your opponent into making weak pawn moves.

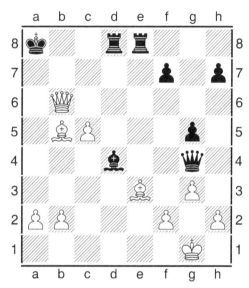

Black to move after 28. Bb5!

<u>**My Favorite Move**</u>   **23. Rxb7+!!**

GAME 23
KNIGHTY KNIGHT!

Alexey Shirov vs. Judit Polgar, Buenos Aires 1994

The Sicilian Defense, Paulsen Variation

The strongest female player of all time is Judit Polgar (b. 1976). The Hungarian phenom has beaten many of the world's best players. She is known for her deadly attacking style, which is energized by very sharp tactics. In the following game against Grandmaster Alexey Shirov (b. 1972), Polgar's amazing knights ride to victory.

1. e4   c5
The Sicilian Defense.

2. Nf3   e6
The Paulsen Variation.

3. d4   cxd4

4. Nxd4   Nc6
Polgar is not afraid to allow the Maróczy Bind.

5. Nc3
But Shirov doesn't play it (5. c4).

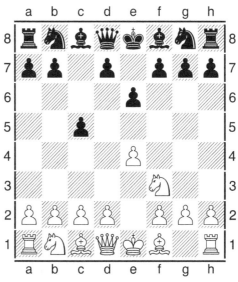

White to move after 2. …e6

5. …d6
Black's pawns now guard a block of squares from c5 to f5.

6. g4
A move popularized by Keres.

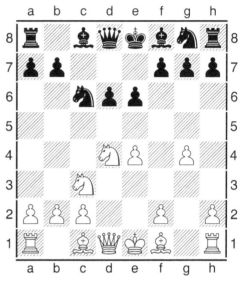

Black to move after 6. g4

6. …a6
It's useful to guard b5, in case Black wants to put her queen on c7.

7. Be3
White develops and strengthens the a7-g1 diagonal.

7. …Nge7
At e7, Black's king-knight supports the knight at c6. But it does block the f8-bishop.

8. Nb3   b5
This move does two things. It makes it possible for the queen-bishop to go to b7, and it also keeps in mind b5-b4.

9. f4
White's line of three pawns on the 4th rank looks threatening.

9. …Bb7
Completing the flank.

10. Qf3
White could also have played 10. Qd2.

10. ...g5!
A pawn sacrifice with a point! Polgar is very aggressive.

11. fxg5
This capture gives up control of e5.

11. ...Ne5
Judit immediately places her knight on this active square.

12. Qg2
White retreats the queen and keeps e4 protected.

12. ...b4
Kicking out the c3-knight.

13. Ne2   h5!
Another interesting pawn sacrifice. Judit has a clever idea in mind.

14. gxh5   Nf5!
The knight is safe because of the b7-bishop's pin. Polgar has terrific knights.

15. Bf2
The bishop retreats to safety.

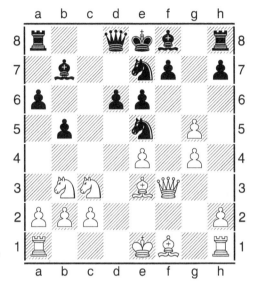

White to move after 11. ...Ne5

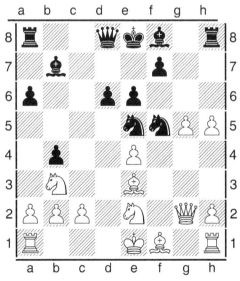

White to move after 14. ...Nf5!

15. ...Qxg5!!
A totally brilliant move!
If 16. Qxg5, Judit has the
knight fork, 16...Nf3+.

16. Na5
Attacking the b7-bishop.

16. ...Ne3!

QUESTION 25: What
happens if 17. Qxg5?

17. Qg3
White couldn't play 17.
Qxg5 because of mate,
thanks to Judit's dancing
knights.

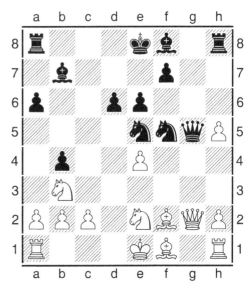

White to move after 15. ...Qxg5!!

17. ...Qxg3
The queen trade wins material.

18. Nxg3   Nxc2+
Black gains the Exchange.

19. Kd1   Nxa1

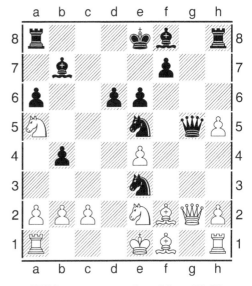

White to move after 16. ...Ne3!

152

20. Nxb7   b3
Judit wisely tries to get
her knight out of the a1
corner.

21. axb3   Nxb3
The knight has gotten out.

22. Kc2   Nc5
Offering a trade.

23. Nxc5
Shirov takes it.

23. ...dxc5

24. Be1
The bishop is going to be
repositioned.

24. ...Nf3

25. Bc3   Nd4+

26. Kd3   Bd6

27. Bg2   Be5
Strengthening d4.

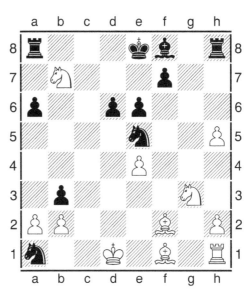

White to move after 20. ...b3

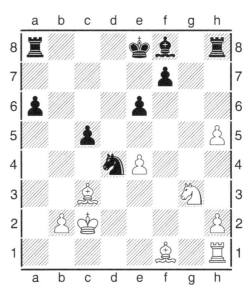

White to move after 25. ...Nd4+

153

28. Kc4   Ke7

Intelligent play. Rather than castle, Black keeps her king in the center for the endgame.

29. Ra1   Nc6

Black's exchange-up position is easily winning.

White resigns (0-1)

White to move after 28. …Ke7

I will always remember Polgar's brilliant use of her knights.

LESSONS LEARNED

* Knights stationed in the center can be monsters.

* An attack on the flank can also attack the center.

* Don't automatically castle if heading to the endgame.

<u>My Favorite Move</u>

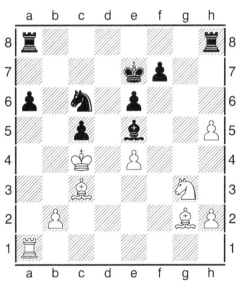

White to move after 29. …Nc6

15. …Qxg5!!

GAME 24
SO CREATIVE

Wesley So vs. Michael Prusikin, Bad Wiesse 2006

The French Defense, Steinitz Variation

Wesley So (b. 1993) is one of the most talented players today. He shows over and over in his games how incredible he is by being very inventive in building his attacks. In this game, Wesley plays Michael Prusikin (b. 1978) and demonstrates how important piece activity really is. Better yet, So does it with artful imagination.

1. e4   e6
The French Defense.

2. d4   d5

3. Nc3   Nf6

4. Bg5
Pinning the knight.

4. ...Be7
Blocking the pin.

5. e5   Nfd7

6. Bxe7
White trades bishops. This is the main line.

6. ...Qxe7

7. f4
Protecting the head pawn.

7. ...a6
Stopping Nb5.

8. Nf3   b6
One reason for b6 is to support c7-c5.

9. Qd2   c5

10. Nd1
Planning c3.

10. ...0-0
Black gets castled.

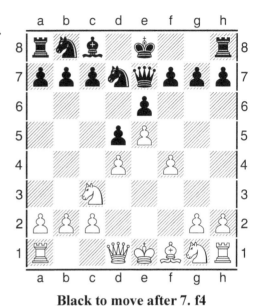

Black to move after 7. f4

11. c3
Supporting the base of the pawn chain.

11. ...f6

12. Bd3
Developing the bishop.

12. ...a5

13. 0-0
Wesley gets castled. He's planning a kingside attack, with the d3-bishop aimed at h7.

13. ...Ba6
Hoping to trade bishops.

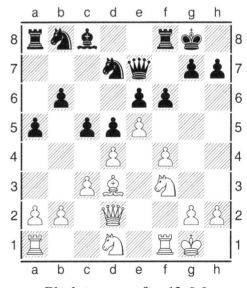

Black to move after 13. 0-0

14. exf6
Opening the e-file.

14. ...Qxf6

15. Ng5
Threatening the h7-pawn.

15. ...g6
Blocking the d3-h7 diagonal.

16. Ne3
Planning Ng4.

16. ...h5
Preventing Ng4. Black is not going to miss that!

17. Rae1
White gets his last inactive piece into play.

17. ...Bxd3
Black trades bishops.

18. Qxd3   cxd4
Black is expecting cxd4, capturing the pawn back.

19. Nxe6!!
But no! So has better plans in mind.

19. ...Qxe6

20. Nxd5
Another sacrifice!

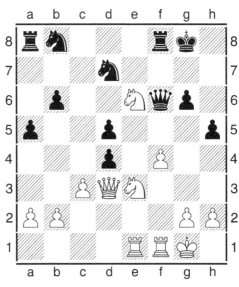

Black to move after 19. Nxe6!!

QUESTION 26: Why can't Black play 20...Qxd5?

20. ...Qf7

21. Re7
Pigging out!

21. ...Qf5
Black is forced to play this move.

22. Qxd4
Capturing the pawn back. Even though So is down material, it doesn't matter because he has a HUGE attack!

22. ...Nf6
Preventing Qg7 mate.

23. Re5
Go away queen.

21. ...Qd7

24. Qd3
Putting pressure on the g6-pawn.

24. ...Nxd5

25. Qxg6+
So doesn't take the knight back. He's *so* creative.

25. ...Qg7

26. Qe6+
Check.

Black to move after 22. Qxd4

158

26. ...Qf7

27. Qh6
Rg5 is coming.

27. ...Qf6
Black tries to stop Rg5.

28. Rg5+
So does it anyway.

28. ...Kf7
Trying to run away.

29. Qh7+   Ke8

30. Rxd5
Doomed. White's queen and rooks will soon force checkmate – an excellent illustration of the power of piece activity.

Black resigns (1-0)

I will always remember
So's two creative sacrifices.

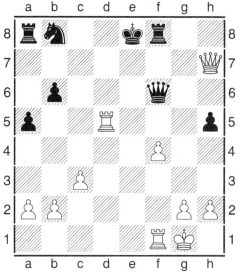

Black to move after 30. Rxd5

LESSONS LEARNED

* Piece activity is often more important than material!

* When attacking, try to use all your pieces.

* So is *so* creative!

My Favorite Move   **19. Nxe6!!**

GAME 25
THE ONLINE IMMORTAL GAME

Magnus Carlsen vs. Anish Giri, Chessable Masters Final 2020

The Queen's Gambit, Semi-Tarrasch Defense

We live in a brave new world. Recently, top players from around the world have found it harder to meet face-to-face, so they've had to compete mainly online. It's easy to think online chess might not be as good as over the board play. But that's not always the case. In fact, the way Magnus Carlsen (b. 1990) handles the attack in this April 27, 2020 game is truly brilliant.

1. d4   Nf6

2. c4   e6

3. Nf3   d5

4. Nc3   c5
This is the move that makes it a Tarrasch Defense. Black strives for open lines and attack.

5. cxd5   Nxd5
Black takes back with a piece to avoid accepting an isolated pawn.

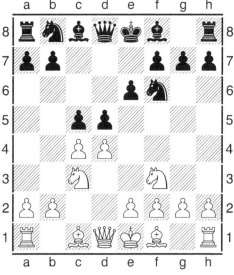

White to move after 4. ....c5

6. e4
White gets his center rolling.

6. ...Nxc3

7. bxc3   cxd4

8. cxd4
White has a mobile pawn center, two pawns vs. one. The correct plan is to mobilize the center at the right time.

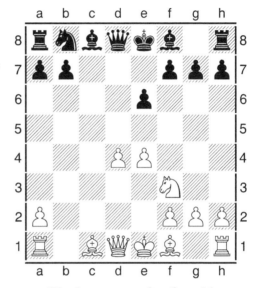

Black to move after 8. cxd4

8. ...Bb4+
Leading to a trade of king-bishop for queen-bishop.

9. Bd2   Bxd2+

10. Qxd2   0–0

11. Bc4
White has more space and slightly greater chances. But with proper play, the game is dynamically equal.

11. ...Nd7
To avoid being pushed on by the d-pawn. However, the knight now has good transfer possibilities.

12. 0–0   b6
Black is going to flank his bishop. He has a queenside pawn majority, but it's not going anywhere yet.

13. Rad1
Centralization.

13. …Bb7
Hitting the White king-pawn.

14. Rfe1
More centralization.

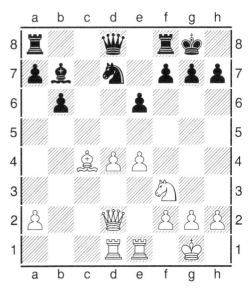

Black to move after 14. Rfe1

14. …Rc8
This is a good file for Black's queen-rook.

15. Bb3   Re8
Black expects the e-file might eventually open.

16. Re3
A rook lift. Where will this rook wind up?

16. …Nf6
A good transfer square. Piling up on e4.

17. d5!
What do you do with a mobile pawn center? You advance it!

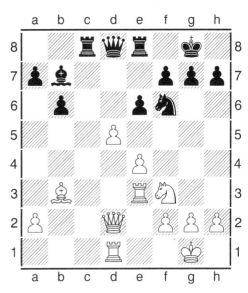

Black to move after 17. d5!

17. …exd5
Opening the e-file.

18. e5!
A nice positional pawn sacrifice. White gets excellent piece play for the pawn.

162

18. ...Ne4

19. Qe1

<u>QUESTION 27</u>: What is White threatening after 19. Qe1?

19. ...Qc7

20. Nd4
An excellent square for the knight.

20. ...a6
Giri had to deal with White's threat to play Nd4-b5.

21. h4!
A bugle call to attack!

<u>QUESTION 28</u>: Can Black just take the e5-pawn for free?

21. ...Rcd8
Black has major pieces on three consecutive files.

22. f3
Forcing the knight to withdraw from the out-post.

22. ...Nc5

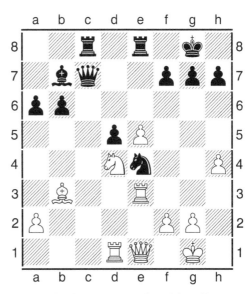

Black to move after 19. Qe1

Black to move after 21. h4!

23. h5
Charge!

23. ...Ne6
Offering a knight trade.

24. Nf5
On f5, the knight is Godzilla.

24. ...d4

25. Red3
Piling up on d4.

25. ...Nc5

26. Rxd4   Rxd4

27. Rxd4   Nxb3
Black now expected 28. axb3.

28. Qg3!
An ingenious *zwischenzug*! Black expected the automatic a2xb3.

28. ...g6
Mate had to be stopped at g7.

29. axb3
Now he can take back.

29. ...Rd8

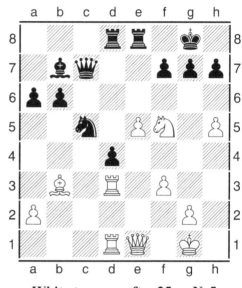

White to move after 25. ...Nc5

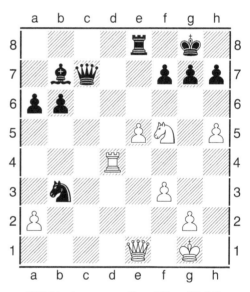

White to move after 27. ...Nxb3

30. e6!!
An incredible discovery!
Now if 30…Qxg3, then
31. Rxd8 is mate.

30. …Qc1+
Black needs to try something.

31. Kh2   Rxd4

32. e7!!
Don't look now, but
White is threatening mate
at e8.

32. …Qc8

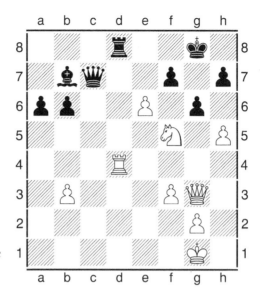

Black to move after 30. e6!!

33. Qe5!!
Now White is threatening two mates.

33. …Rh4+

34. Kg3
There is no defense. An
unbelievable game!

Black resigns (1–0)

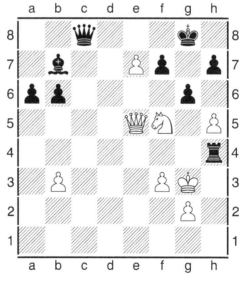

Black to move after 34. Kg3

I will always remember Carlsen's mind-blowing *zwischenzug*.

<u>**LESSONS LEARNED**</u>

* Don't play automatically.

* Don't trade good pieces for bad.

* Don't play Magnus Carlsen when he's on a roll.

<u>**My Favorite Move**</u>   **33. Qe5!!**

GLOSSARY

Term	Definition
Capablanca's Rule	when activating a pawn majority, push the unopposed pawn first
Centralization	improving a piece by putting it in the center
Clearance	moving a piece or pawn to make a square or line available
Combination	a tactical series with at least two moves
Constriction	keeping a player cramped
Cutoff	a barrier created by a queen or rook
Decoy	an outside passed pawn, used to lure away the opposing king
Deflection	distracting a piece or a pawn to gain material

Desperado	getting something for a lost piece
Development	getting a piece into action
Discovered attack	moving a piece or pawn to uncover an attack from behind
Fianchetto	developing a bishop on the side, to its knight-two square, aiming it at the center
File	a vertical row on the chessboard
Fork	attacking two or more enemy units with one friendly unit
Frontier line	imaginary line dividing the board in half horizontally
Half-open file	a file with pawns only of one color
Hole	a weak square inviting attack and occupation
In-between move	an unexpected move played before completing a sequence started earlier
Initiative	control of play
Isolani	an isolated pawn

Isolated pawn	a pawn with no friendly pawns to either side of it
Little center	each side has one pawn in the center, one on its 3rd rank vs. one on its 4th rank
Luft	escape square for the king
Major piece	queen or a rook
Material	pieces and pawns
Minor piece	a bishop or a knight
Open file	a file with no pawns on it
Outpost	strong, occupiable square across the frontier line
Pawn chain	interlocked black and white pawns
Pawn grab-bing	taking a risky pawn
Pawn majority	in any sector of the board, having more pawns than your opponent
Pig	a rook on the opponent's 2nd rank

Pin	line attack preventing a piece or pawn from moving off the line
Quiet move	a useful move that doesn't check or capture
Rank	a horizontal row on the chessboard
Rook lift	transferring a rook up a file to shift across a rank
Skewer	a line attack that forces an opposing piece to move away, exposing a piece behind to capture
Strategy	general plans and goals
Strongpoint	a solid pawn that can support a piece
Tactics	specific attacks and combinations
Tempo	a move
The Exchange	rook for minor piece
Transpose	change the move order and get to the same place; change one opening into another
Waiting move	a move played to make it be the opponent's turn

Weak square	a square that cannot be guarded by a pawn
Zugzwang	a situation where moving worsens the player's own position
Zwischenzug	an unexpected move played before completing a sequence started earlier

ANSWERS TO QUESTIONS

QUESTION 1: Why does Black play 7...Nh5?

ANSWER 1: Black hopes to win the Exchange by 8...Ng3+.

QUESTION 2: What happens if 4...dxe5 instead?

ANSWER 2: White wins a pawn by 5. Qxd8+ Kxd8 6. Nxe5.

QUESTION 3: How would White have answered 14...Nf7?

ANSWER 3: By trapping the bishop with 15. c5.

QUESTION 4: What follows after 23...axb6?

ANSWER 4: 24. cxb6, attacking the queen and threatening mate.

QUESTION 5: Does Black take the advantage after 9...Nxc3 10. bxc3 Bxc3?

ANSWER 5: No! White is better after 11. Qb3.

QUESTION 6: Can White safely take the rook?

ANSWER 6: No! If White takes the rook, he gets mated at g2.

QUESTION 7: Why can't White simply take the Black queen?

ANSWER 7: Either White gets mated (24. hxg3 Ne2#; or 24. fxg3 Ne2+ 25. Kh1 Rxf1#) or he winds up a knight down after 24. Qxg3 Ne2+ 25. Kh1 Nxg3+ 26. Kg1 Ne2+ 27. Kh1, and the rook at h3 moves to safety.

QUESTION 8: Why does White play 6. Qxd4 instead of 6. Nxd4?

ANSWER 8: White wants to avoid 6. Nxd4 c5, when White will lose the right to castle next move.

QUESTION 9: What happens on 29. Kxf4?

ANSWER 9: Black skewers the Exchange by 29...Bg5+.

QUESTION 10: What does 10...Bd7 suggest about Black's castling plans?

ANSWER 10: Black plans to castle queenside.

QUESTION 11: If 17...Qe7 18. Bb5, can Black safely play 18...Nxb4?

ANSWER 11: No! White wins the knight by 19. Rb1.

QUESTION 12: What happens after 18...Ng6?

ANSWER 12: White plays 19. Nh6+, busting up Black's kingside.

QUESTION 13: Would 23. Rc5 have been better?

ANSWER 13: No! That would fail to 23...Bxd4+.

QUESTION 14: Why didn't Black play 29...Re4?

ANSWER 14: On 29...Re4, there follows 30. Bxg7 Bxg7 31. f6.

QUESTION 15: Why didn't White take the knight, 21. Rxd4?

ANSWER 15: If he takes the knight, he gets mated at c1.

QUESTION 16: Why did White play 35. Kg1?
ANSWER 16: To avoid Bf8-d6.

QUESTION 17: Why might 14. Rad1 be safer than Rfd1?

ANSWER 17: It doesn't weaken the square f2.

QUESTION 18: What happens if Black captures the pawn *en passant*, 10...exf3?

ANSWER 18: White plays 11. Qxf5+, winning a bishop.

QUESTION 19: Does Black win a piece by 11...exf4 12. Bxf4 g5?

ANSWER 19: No! 13. e5! gives White favorable complications.

QUESTION 20: What happens after 6...Ng4?

ANSWER 20: It loses material to 7. Bb5+.

QUESTION 21: How does play continue after
11. 0-0-0?

ANSWER 21: Black wins a piece by 11...Nxd4
12. Qxd4 Ng4.

QUESTION 22: What does 14. Rad1 threaten?

ANSWER 22: It threatens 15. dxc5, followed by
16. Bxh7+!

QUESTION 23: What happens if Black now plays 19...Bd7?

ANSWER 23: White wins the Exchange by 20. Ba3.

QUESTION 24: What happens after 24...Kc7?

ANSWER 24: White mates by 25. Qa7+ Kc8 26. Ba6#.

QUESTION 25: What happens if 17. Qxg5?

ANSWER 25: Black mates by 17...Nf3#.

QUESTION 26: Why can't Black play 20...Qxd5?

ANSWER 26: If 20...Qxd5, then 21. Qxg6+ demolishes Black.

QUESTION 27: What is White threatening after 19. Qe1?

ANSWER 27: White threatens 20. Rxe4.

QUESTION 28: Can Black just take the e5-pawn for free?

ANSWER 28: No! The advance f2-f3 would win material.

PHOTOS

Oliver attends the North American Youth Chess Championships in Mexico. At this tournament, he competed against players from the United States, Canada, and Mexico. November, 2018

Oliver gets ready for some chess at the legendary Marshall Chess Club in New York City's Greenwich Village. May, 2018

Oliver and his chess coach NM Bruce Pandolfini prepare before the next round of competition at the 2019 National Elementary (K-6) Championship in Nashville. May, 2019

Oliver was crowned New York City Champion at the Kasparov Greater
New York Scholastic Chess Championships. February, 2017

Oliver flies out of the Galápagos Islands en route to the Pan American Youth Chess Championships in Guayaquil, Ecuador. July, 2019

Oliver, at home in New York City, displays his collection of chess boards.
His favorites include a board signed by World Chess Champion Garry
Kasparov and another autographed by the U.S. Chess Champion Fabia-
no Caruana. September, 2018

On a break from playing chess, Oliver leaps into the air in Cape Cod. June, 2020

Oliver receives a medal at the 2019 National K-12 Grade Championships in Orlando. He played the 4th Grade Championship Section and tied for 2nd place with a nail-biting win in the seventh round, lasting over three-and-a-half hours. December, 2019

Oliver finished first in his quad at the Charity Chess Championship in New York City. His prize was a chess board personally signed by numerous chess Grandmasters who had attended the fundraising event. May, 2017

Oliver gets ready to play chess at the World Cadet Chess Championship in Weifang, China. August, 2019

Oliver visits the magnificent Tian Tan Buddha (Big Buddha) in Hong Kong, one of the largest seated Buddhas in the world. August, 2019

Oliver takes a break between chess rounds, with NM Bruce Pandolfini (left) and FM Mike Klein (right) at the 2019 National Elementary (K-6) Championships, held at the Gaylord Opryland Resort and Convention Center in Nashville. May, 2019

Oliver claims his very big trophy at the 2015 National K-12 Grade Championships in Orlando. He played in the Kindergarten Championship Section and became a National Champion at five years old. December, 2015

Oliver engages in another of his passions, soccer! Here he is playing for his travel soccer team in New York City. May, 2018

Oliver attracts a crowd of onlookers in New York City's Union Square, as he practices his moves against players many times his size. March, 2017

Bring it! Oliver faces his next opponent at the New York State Scholastic Chess Championships in Saratoga Springs. March, 2018

When Oliver was five years old, he wanted to be a subway conductor when he grew up. He achieved his goal of riding every single subway line in New York City, including the obscure ones that only operate during rush hours. June, 2017

Oliver gets ready to enter the venue for the World Cadet Chess Championship in Weifang, China. August, 2019

Oliver with GM Maurice Ashley and GM Irina Krush at the Charity Chess Championship in New York City. May, 2018

Oliver takes in the Pacific Ocean during a break from competition at the
North American Youth Chess Championships in Mexico. November, 2018

SPECIAL THANKS

After finishing this, my first book, I checked my work carefully, reading through the manuscript again and again, looking for mistakes and better ways to say things. My mother also read it thoroughly – every period, comma, sentence, and chess move – and she had valuable advice on various aspects of the document. But she is not an advanced chess player who could judge the worth of certain analytic comments. To that end, I am thankful to International Master John Donaldson, America's leading chess historian. He had several important suggestions, for which I am most appreciative.

I would like to recognize Andrew Im, my mother's dear friend. Not only did he provide excellent advice, he connected me to my publisher, Metabook.

Finally, I would like to thank everyone at Metabook Entertainment – especially Benjamin Alfonsi and Ken Siman – for their vision and creativity, for believing in this book, and for believing in me. They and their incredibly talented team have been absolutely amazing. Without Metabook, I might not have made the right moves.

ABOUT THE AUTHOR

Oliver Boydell was born in New York City to a Vietnamese mother and an English father. A National Chess Champion and a New York City Chess Champion, Oliver developed a passion for chess at the age of five. He started competing in chess tournaments during the same year and is a regular contender at New York City, New York State, and National Scholastic Chess Championships. Oliver endeavors to become a chess Grandmaster. He loves sports, especially playing soccer and skiing down double black runs with his older brother Sebastien. Oliver is ten years old and lives in New York City with his family. You can visit him at www.oliverboydell.com.

CPSIA information can be obtained
at www.ICGtesting.com
Printed in the USA
BVHW031533171220
595871BV00004B/32